D1232279

PRAISE FOR
THE ANSWERS ARE THERE

"*The Answers Are There: Building Peace from the Inside Out* shares a lived example of what's possible when you honor the resources of people working together in community. In powerful, vivid stories, Libby Hoffman shows us the transformation that can be unleashed when ordinary people are supported to fulfill their vision for themselves and their communities."

–Leymah Gbowee, 2011 Nobel Peace Prize laureate

"Libby Hoffman has poured out her huge and beautiful heart into the stunning and riveting pages of this book. The work she has done and the way she describes it in this truly remarkable account will break open your heart and your capacity to see the profound dignity of people who go through unimaginable suffering. The teaching stories in this book are astonishing and vital to us all. Read this and learn how to have the world we want."

–Lynne Twist, author of *The Soul of Money*

"*The Answers Are There* is a much-needed book in today's world, where we seek a greater dignity of purpose and practice, the deepening of more respectful relationships, and creativity in the pursuit of peace and development. This book offers a rare gift: Libby Hoffman's journey of both personal growth and systemic transformation, as experienced in the world of philanthropy and social change. She opens a window into the integrity required to face and follow the questions that unfold from our deepest commitments—and the stories of her life work offer better pathways of integrity for us all."

—John Paul Lederach, professor emeritus,
University of Notre Dame

"In this luminous and powerful, gorgeously written book, Libby Hoffman challenges us to create a peacebuilding system based on wholeness and dignity, rather than fragmentation and loss. Hoffman shows us how communities made peace in Sierra Leone, woven from their traditions, driven by women, and accepting that even the most violent perpetrators could become 'good somebodies.' *The Answers Are There* brings us nothing short of a new architecture for peace, steeped in the wisdom of an actual process that healed a nation unraveled by war."

—Melanie Greenberg, managing director of
peacebuilding, Humanity United

"Libby Hoffman's rejection of traditional 'black and white' thinking is a clarion call for the peace and security sector. As her book demonstrates in clear, concrete, and human ways, the only way to achieve lasting peace is by embracing complex thinking and by trusting and supporting local people. The people in our field need to read this book and take up its invitation to transform ourselves."

–Alexandra Toma, executive director,
Peace and Security Funders Group

"The indigenous restorative justice and reconciliation process that Libby Hoffman and John Caulker pioneered not only helped a nation confront its painful past; it also reconstructed communal relationships that successfully stemmed the tide of the Ebola virus and paved the way for the national government's innovative, participatory model of local development. Libby Hoffman's book offers a powerful story of a people's self-determination to recover, repair, and reconcile after war—in ways nothing short of transformative."

–Carl Stauffer, PhD, senior expert for reconciliation,
United States Institute of Peace

"This book, and the story of Fambul Tok it explores, challenges the global tendency to see peacebuilding as a technocratic, outsider-driven activity. Libby offers an antidote to the world of metrics, consultants, and top-down funders, inviting the reader instead to connect with themselves and the humanness of others and transform violence through listening, nurturing, co-creating, and sharing. Truly inspiring."

–Professor Brandon Hamber, John Hume & Tip O'Neill chair in peace, Ulster University

THE ANSWERS
ARE THERE

BUILDING PEACE
FROM THE INSIDE OUT

THE
ANSWERS
ARE
THERE

LIBBY HOFFMAN
FOREWORD BY **CLARE LOCKHART**

BLUE CHAIR
PRESS

Published by Blue Chair Press
Saco, ME
www.catalystforpeace.org

Copyright © 2022 Libby Hoffman

All rights reserved.

Thank you for purchasing an authorized edition of this book and for
complying with copyright law. No part of this book may be reproduced,
stored in a retrieval system, or transmitted by any means, electronic,
mechanical, photocopying, recording, or otherwise, without written
permission from the copyright holder.

For permission to reproduce copyrighted material, grateful
acknowledgment is made to the following:
David Whyte, "Everything is Waiting for You" from *River Flow: New &
Selected Poems*. Copyright © 2019 David Whyte. Excerpt reprinted with
permission from Many Rivers Press, Langley, WA.

Distributed by River Grove Books

Design and composition by Greenleaf Book Group
Cover design by theBookDesigners
Cover art ©Shutterstock/kotoffei; ©Shutterstock/HstrongART

Publisher's Cataloging-in-Publication data is available.

Print ISBN: 979-8-9862030-1-0

eBook ISBN: 979-8-9862030-0-3

First Edition

for
Marcia Payne Hoffman,
Earline Young Payne,
Frances Adelia DeTurk Young,
and all our mothers' mothers' mothers

Yesterday I was clever,
So I wanted to change the world.
Today I am wise, so I am
Changing myself.

—Rumi

CONTENTS

FOREWORD

When I first joined the government in 2018, Sierra Leone was on edge following a divisive national election. We were still reeling from the Ebola outbreak of 2014–2015, coupled with the legacy of our 11-year civil war, especially in rural communities, which saw so much violence. We thus saw that there was a demonstrated need for us as a nation to continue to consolidate the hard-won peace and strengthen our cohesion as a country.

We saw great hope and possibility for social cohesion and local development in a new initiative emerging from civil society, an initiative that we would implement as the Wan Fambul National Framework for Inclusive Governance and Local Development. This community development framework, born out of a unique collaboration between government and civil society, over which I now superintend, brings planning down to the grassroots level, in the village and the chiefdom. The Framework ensures that our country's development is inclusive, led and owned by the people.

Through the Wan Fambul process, communities establish their own priorities, ask for guidance and support, and forge ahead under their *own* leadership, rather than wait for aid initiatives or donor checks, as has prevailed in the past.

The Wan Fambul National Framework sparks energy, imagination, and resources that are already within people and communities; it creates inclusive spaces that allow people to lead, not just in name but in practice. It gives special attention to women's leadership and to social cohesion. The People's Planning Process, the community mobilization program that grounds this framework, is specifically designed to include voices that have hitherto been left out of governance and create space for them to be part of the identification of community priorities and needed resources. It empowers communities and individuals by inviting and supporting people's participation through inclusive structures at the sectional, chiefdom, and district levels. These structures have been used to address conflict, natural disasters, the Ebola virus, and the current COVID-19 pandemic in unique and innovative ways.

We know as Sierra Leoneans that our ordinary citizens—particularly in the rural areas—are capable of great leadership when given the opportunity. The People's Planning Process proved this again and again. In one community, residents contributed fifteen cents a week, for 18 months, to begin the construction of a bridge. This was not simply a small footpath; from their own pockets and with their own leadership, they established four concrete pillars for a major modern flyover. The local and national governments supported their initiative, and a community once cut off completely during the rainy season now enjoys easier and cheaper transportation, more trade opportunities, and better health outcomes for pregnant women. Stories like this repeated themselves across the pilot districts of the People's Planning Process, as villagers established community farms, built new health outposts, and contributed to education of the least well-off.

Across Sierra Leone, there are stories that exemplify the power of people-centered development from the most local level. It is at this local level where people have so much energy for constructive activity on behalf of one another and their communities, and where trusted channels of engagement and support can be established with significant impact. The success of our country's development depends upon the level of trust within and between our communities. Indeed, it is clear to us, from our lived experience, that trust is the cornerstone of resilience. The Framework, and the process it was built on, helps us nurture and strengthen that trust.

The Wan Fambul National Framework came out of 13 years of fieldwork by Fambul Tok, a Sierra Leonean nongovernmental organization working in partnership with Catalyst for Peace. The Government of Sierra Leone has incorporated the Framework into Sierra Leone's National Development Plan 2019–2023 as a priority and a flagship program. We are creating new inclusive governance structures at the chiefdom, district, and national levels to support and sustain it, and adapting our local governance and decentralization acts and policies accordingly. The ongoing work inside and outside government to implement the Framework holistically and comprehensively represents a new era not only for development, but for relations between government and civil society. As in so many other development contexts, the relationship between government and civil society can be fraught, and mistrust can grow between them. In working together to design and implement a national framework based on the work of civil society, government leaders and civil society leaders have forged new bonds and found new, mutually beneficial ways of working that benefit all Sierra Leoneans.

The government and people of Sierra Leone are rising to the challenge of doing development differently in order to meet our needs and fulfill our potential, on our terms. We invite the world to learn from our experience and example.

—The Honorable Francess Piagie Alghali
Minister of State
Office of the Vice President
Government of Sierra Leone

FOREWORD

I n the spring of 2002, in a remote part of Herat Province in western Afghanistan, I met several dozen people who had just returned from exile—families now living together with their livestock under tents of animal skin propped up by branches. These families needed shelter, food, medical support, and income in order to rebuild their lives. The traditional aid response to these needs would be a panoply of resources brought in from the outside: bags of imported wheat, teams of foreign doctors with imported medicines, and dozens of other "humanitarians"—United Nations and international nongovernmental organization workers in expensive white 4x4s.

This small community returned in the midst of a humanitarian emergency, which was drawing a huge influx of international aid. Big humanitarian agencies were planning to impose thousands of projects, but an alternative approach already existed. Only days after I arrived to work with the UN, I came across a team of humanitarians who were taking a different approach to the challenges facing communities like that group of returned Afghans—an approach that entrusted them to make their own decisions. The program they established gave communities a block grant to use however they saw fit.

A few weeks into this work, when my colleagues and I visited some of the communities that had received this type of grant, people were eager to tell us about how they were faring. This feeling of being trusted—something that had so far eluded them in their experiences both as refugees abroad and as returnees at home— was far more valuable than handouts, they told us. And they were excited to have discovered their collective capabilities: One of them could read and write and offered to teach all the children. Another could work with animal skins to sell in the market. Another had access to a truck and could deliver products into town. "When we first came back, we were stuck and didn't know how we could get started," one of them said. Their authority over their block grant inspired them to identify and organize around other resources they already had—resources that came from who they were and how they had experienced the world—and an emerging sense of common purpose stirred them to activity.

In this encounter, and many others like it, I learned lessons that have stayed with me in my decades of work in international development. First, the real resources aren't the money and projects from abroad or the experts with expensive degrees brought into communities from outside. Second, it didn't take much to catalyze their efforts or honor their agency. If international organizations could hold back from *deciding for* communities and instead allow them to claim space as experts on what needs to be done, those communities could come together and decide on their own priorities.

The third lesson I learned has become a bedrock principle of my work: being trusted acknowledged people's dignity, allowing them to be seen and to lead as people of powerful capability. Across the world, people lament a loss of trust in institutions, but very little attention is paid to the importance of placing trust in *people*—entrusting them to identify their own priorities, make their own decisions, and chart their own paths toward realizing their hopes for their communities and for themselves.

Communities around the world express and enact these ambitions frequently—and often without wider recognition, let alone direct support, from international actors. In Venezuela, as the national economy collapsed, local communities organized community kitchens and food distribution. In Colombia, in the middle of a war, cooperation between communities and local businesses delivered essential services. In Nepal, local self-help groups in water, schooling, and health kept essential services running during the years of war. In Puerto Rico, in the aftermath of Hurricane Maria, communities identified assets that could attract investment in the future tourism industry. There are so many other examples around the world—in India, in Sri Lanka, in Yemen, in Morocco, in Russia, in Spain, and in the United States, where the coronavirus pandemic yielded myriad examples of neighborhood-centered recovery programs.

These programs build upon a long history of global learning and exchange. In Pakistan, I was inspired to learn that a successful program dedicated to tackling poverty, which reached thousands of villages in the most remote parts of the country, had its conceptual roots in the thinking of a 19th-century German mayor named Raiffeisen, who believed in the power of local communities' capacities to lift themselves out of poverty through self-help and self-governance. He helped pioneer a system of rural cooperatives and credit unions that still thrives today. A countrywide community program in Indonesia provided lifesaving support after an economic crisis, and its success inspired other policymakers in the region, from the Philippines and Laos to Timor-Leste. Informal webs of connection—of learning and yearning—unite the world, catalyzing creativity, problem-solving, and community renewal in places and ways too often overlooked.

These webs of connection exist at every level—including across local communities. In Afghanistan, I watched magic happen under the tent at the National Convention of Communities, an anchor of the countrywide community development process. When they convened to share their priorities and problems, people from different parts of the country realized they had the same issues: How do you keep livestock healthy in the face of disease? How do you prepare for seasons of unusually intensive drought? The recognition of common challenges—and the expansive community knowledge, capability, and resources available to tackle them—catalyzed ever more creative ways of innovating, and scaling, common approaches to problem-solving.

Despite so many examples, contemporary and historical, of how communities successfully nurture and (re)build themselves, the real power of community agency often remains invisible and unsupported in our international system. International actors speak about the principles of "local ownership" frequently, but we have yet to follow our words with our actions, especially when those are expressed through our programming. Creating the spaces for real ownership, whether in a village or across a country, takes longer, but it is the only way real *community* transformation can take root.

At its core, community-led development isn't about changing the local; it is about changing the way international peacebuilding and development works. In Indonesia, for example, it took the financial crisis of 1997–1998 for international donors to take the leap and trust people in the villages. By that point, they had little choice: there was no alternative when it came to getting resources to villages at scale. Two decades on, this approach is now the foundation for village development in the country.

In Afghanistan, using tens of thousands of UN and NGO projects to reach villagers might have seemed like the best way of tracking whether donor money reached the places it was meant for, but the improved accountability that international actors supposedly offered was illusory. In a village in Afghanistan's central highlands, residents told me how they became forensic accountants, investigating where the $150 million allocated to their region by a UN agency had gone; they were shocked to find out that most of it had disappeared in layers of overhead expenses, leaving only enough money for wooden beams they couldn't use in their village. This capacity to track and account for funding can be created at a national scale: I have seen villages in many countries set up verifiable tracking and reporting systems that allow for detailed accountability down to the smallest expenditures. This type of tracking can become the basis for development programs with much higher accountability levels than the current ways of working.

We are in a unique moment of potential: The entire international system is reexamining its ways of working. And there are many examples of better practice. In the aftermath of conflict in Nepal in the early 2000s, development partners did not rush in with their quick-impact projects and humanitarian assistance. Instead, they took a step back and allowed civil society actors to chart their own socioeconomic plans and programs, around which they then built their own support. Citizens took initiative in every sector: the media created more space for solution-oriented discussions rather than criticism; industrialists put savings into youth training programs; local NGOs focused their energies on working alongside community programs to expand service delivery; and political groups agreed on a common program of action instead of being stymied by gridlock. While huge challenges remain in Nepal, enough consensus was created to bring key actors together to tackle some important issues.

Approaching development through listening and entrusting people to make decisions is far less costly than the vast and cumbersome infrastructures of the international aid system. And we have seen, over and over again, that it is more successful and more sustainable. Today, there is an urgency to build on these lessons with a new approach to international development. If international actors are meant—and able—to support rather than undermine the healing of societies after conflict; to honor the space for democratic decision-making; and to nurture individuals to grow their families, livelihoods, and neighborhoods, this approach—beginning our work with the belief that *the answers are there*—is foundational.

And this book is where we can begin. Libby Hoffman's book, the story of her decade-plus of work with Sierra Leonean human rights activist John Caulker, shows us how reconnecting communities after violence can create the momentum to tackle deeply rooted development challenges. Her way of working shows the value of long-term commitment to listening and understanding; it teaches us how to question our assumptions. Her personal journey exemplifies how an international partner can accompany rather than impose, listening rather than assuming a position of expertise. Libby's narrative begins in courage and conviction of experience. Rooted in a belief that "it doesn't have to be this way," her book shares a working model of just that: a new way of working. It is an inspirational call into a new paradigm, and I hope you will join me in answering that call.

—Clare Lockhart
Director, Institute for State Effectiveness
Author, *Fixing Failed States*

Memory can be creative. As I've been writing this book, I've been surprised by that. I find unexpected memories coming to me, and my reflections on them unleash new creative sparks. As I find new learning from old experiences, I wonder if those lessons, those ideas, have an agency of their own, since it seems they almost want to be part of my thinking and imagining forward, part of the fertile soil in which my being and my work unfold their next layer. That's happened for me often enough that I think my soul must have its own knowledge of how to reach me, how to awaken me to its desire. Sometimes it whispers. Sometimes it yells. Sometimes it knocks persistently until, annoyed, I open the door and explore.

Or is it imagination that sometimes comes to my awareness as memory? A future—or a present?—so impossible to perceive with the analytical mind that it dresses up as something familiar, something it knows I will welcome, and then sneaks in through the back door?

I suspect you have your own soul-whispers. I offer these reflections in the hope that they help you hear and listen to your own soul's voice, which I know is sometimes not easy. I suspect my own whispers are part of a larger whispering

*echoing through our world—a part of our collective uncon-
scious, awakening, wanting us to listen and receive. If enough
of us welcome the whispers, if we listen, absorb, and share,
perhaps we can seed the soil of our collective consciousness
and see new growth bloom.*

*Imagination is calling. This story is my lived response to
imagination's call, which is ongoing. May this book open you
to yours and help you respond.*

OPENING

The first time I visited Kpoundu, on the far-eastern edge of Sierra Leone, just steps from the Guinean border, the dusty village appeared largely deserted. Most of its thatched-roof mud huts stood silent, grim reminders of the deaths within their walls. Just a year before, Ebola had ravaged first this village, then the whole country. "Everyone in that house died," a resident told me. "And in that one next to it. And the one next to that . . ." It was the summer of 2015, eight years into my work supporting postwar reconciliation in Sierra Leone, and I had seen countless times that people were more than the tragedies they experienced. But that day in Kpoundu, it was difficult not to feel overwhelmed. Ebola had killed 22 people in this tiny village—half of its population—and 80 more in nearby villages. Over the course of 14 months, more than 14,000 people across the country had become sick, and close to 4,000 had died, a depth of loss people could explain only by reaching for comparisons to their civil war, two decades before.

And yet, on that hot July day, I also saw something else. At the edge of town, several dozen women gathered under the shade of large mango trees, many with infants on their backs or at their breasts, or small children playing near their feet. These women had walked to Kpoundu from 16 neighboring villages, an all-day trek for some, to discuss how they wanted to rebuild their communities after Ebola. Their conversation was as lively as their clothing, a glorious array of vivid colors and patterns. They bubbled over with generous words of affirmation and support for each other and for the ideas they shared, and their keen, attentive listening equally spoke volumes.

Delicious smells wafted as giant pots of rice and stew were prepared nearby for everyone, giving the event a festive, family feel. The noise grew louder and livelier as the women discussed and decided what projects they could take on together, and how they wanted to help their communities with the money they would make.

The Peace Mothers, as they came to call themselves, were bucking decades-long patterns in international aid. They refused to let labels like "poor," "war-ravaged," and "Ebola-devastated" define them, and they rejected the status quo of humanitarian aid, which consigned them to wait for outsiders to come help them, if help ever came. Instead, the women organized to work together with what they already had for the good of their whole region, and judging from the animated participation, that invitation was awakening a powerful resource for their communal welfare.

They decided first to make and sell soap, and with that began a cooperative venture that is still growing. They have since built community centers with the money they made, given their children access to education, and prevented election violence. Their leaders now advise the district on peace and development and teach other districts how to strengthen community leadership.

But when outsiders look at Kpoundu, what do we see? Do we see the village primarily in terms of what has happened *to* it—the challenges its people have faced and the problems they have? Or do we see their resources and potential, the capacity that is present within the community, even if not yet visible to us, ready to be invited into action and expression?

The "we" I refer to here are predominantly Western, or Western-trained, international peace and development workers. Whatever our personal backgrounds, we are professionalized and acculturated into a system that divides those with needs from those with resources, assigning narrow, mutually exclusive definitions of both. The system labels communities dealing with violence, poverty, or weak governance as those having "needs," while outsiders are those with the resources and expertise who come to help. This deficit-based lens has a totalizing effect, making it more difficult to see, much less build on, the resources and potential *already present* within communities "in need." This way of seeing supports a hierarchy built into the status quo: international experts are at the "top" of a system of knowledge, capacity, and resources, and local communities are at the bottom. The system we were trained to work in envisions aid as a one-directional flow from those with expertise and resources to those with needs, further entrenching the dichotomy.

The system also dichotomizes *us as people*. No matter where you are in the system, its logic insists that change happens "over there"—externally, often in faraway places, and always outside of oneself. Analytical skill and abstract thinking are privileged over the wisdom of lived experience and the power of the local—of care, of community, and of home. The system says that people can't be trusted to solve their own problems; it reduces power to the capacity to control an outcome rather than the ability to liberate potential for good and to nourish mutual flourishing.

This is a book about how to unmake that system.

In my 35 years of experience, including 20 running my own granting and operating foundation, I have learned a lot about how to undo the entanglements of the system-as-it-has-always-been, and about how to build and inhabit something better. As a white American woman trained in the mindsets that underpin the status quo, I've had to learn how to unmake the thought patterns I've inherited so that I can live out my commitment to working differently. This critical self-reflection was exponentially fast-tracked when I came into $20 million in my late thirties (much more on that throughout the book). Suddenly, I was able to both create and fund programming to embody my highest values. And immediately, I ran into another dichotomy embedded within the status quo: the division between funders and practitioners. I rebelled against that false choice. I wanted to be both.

I wanted to create and work in ongoing, genuine, co-creative partnership with people coded by the status quo as "local beneficiaries." I wanted the mutuality of offering and learning in partnership, in a two-directional flow, built on relationships of mutual trust and thriving. I wanted to look for, magnify, and help grow local communities' knowledge and resources in organic and iterative ways. I wanted programming that valued analytical reasoning but also carved channels for things like imagination and vision and creativity. I wanted to see and serve not only outwardly visible accomplishments but also an ongoing, inward deepening of purpose and clarity of calling—for myself and for others. And I wanted a space in which I could learn as much as I might teach, receive as much as I might give.

In this book, I'm going to show you how I've built that kind of system, in practice, over time.

Peace from the inside out

The story of Kpoundu's Peace Mothers is not an isolated one; it happened as part of a systematic effort to build peace and development from the inside out, led by the Sierra Leonean nongovernmental organization Fambul Tok. Fifteen years ago, I began a partnership with John Caulker, a Sierra Leonean human rights advocate, and we started Fambul Tok (Krio for "family talk") to create space for community healing, using indigenous restorative justice traditions, after the country's 11-year civil war. Our animating purpose wasn't to solve problems, to "save" communities, or even to meet needs, per se. Rather, we grounded our work in the intention of *fulfilling potential*. We sought to create space for people and communities—and, ultimately, the country—to identify, claim, and fulfill the potential we believed was always there, even after the devastation of war.

From that taproot, the tree of community healing burst forth and flourished. Over its first seven years, the Fambul Tok staff facilitated close to 250 tradition-based community bonfire ceremonies of truth-telling, apology, and forgiveness across six districts in Sierra Leone. The ceremonies involved more than 2,500 villages, and more than 4,500 people testified to more than 150,000 of their neighbors. We saw communities come together to face difficult truths and find their way forward. In the process, we saw individual and communal hearts made whole, and we saw this wholeness animate local agency and capacity. Communities came alive again as tens of thousands of people re-membered their cultural and communal riches—riches still there after war—and drew upon those resources to reconcile and then lead their own recovery.

After every village reconciliation bonfire, the communities would designate a Peace Tree where they could gather to address new issues that arose. They formed Peace Mothers groups for women to continue to heal while working together for their communities. They rekindled the practice of community farming and used the proceeds to support local development. Individual healing and reanimated community went hand in hand.

We also saw how truth-telling and forgiveness in these communities, shared through a feature-length documentary I produced, opened imagination and conversation around the world—about the power of community and about what is possible when we look for, claim, and live into our wholeness, even in the middle of brokenness. These stories are still reaching and inspiring people today, sparking new ideas around restorative justice, forgiveness, and healing after atrocity.

Through it all, John and I (and our organizations) lived out a system of peace and development the way we felt that system should be. We eschewed the neocolonial grooves of the dominant humanitarian system and instead forged a path and process rooted in wholeness and mutuality, engaged over time with and through committed relationships and networks of care, from the most local to the national and international levels.

By the time Ebola struck, six years after our first reconciliation ceremony, we had seeded a network of strengthened communities across Sierra Leone. We confronted Ebola with the same approach that we had brought to confronting the past. When we encountered national and international responses that ignored or worked against community leadership, even while using language to the contrary, we responded by building and advocating for a connected national network of support instead—one that built bridges from local communities to national policy and carried community voices into the national response to Ebola in meaningful ways.

Based on our success at community-led reconciliation, we challenged prevailing global norms of crisis response and recovery that ignore local capacity and perpetuate colonial, outside-in dynamics. Step by step, we built a process for people and communities to lead their own recovery from Ebola and take charge of their ongoing development. We built connections from local communities to local government and then to policymakers at the national level, ensuring that Sierra Leonean citizens themselves led the process. As a result, people and communities could ask for what they needed and wanted, work together with their local leaders to achieve their vision, and build government connections to help that work be effective.

Seeing such vivid examples of success, the government of Sierra Leone decided to build a crucial national policy around this people- and community-centered approach, birthing the Wan Fambul National Framework for Inclusive Governance and Local Development. The government is now working to implement the Framework nationwide while building the inclusive national infrastructure to support and sustain it. And Sierra Leone's example is in turn inspiring a global network of policymakers and practitioners who are committed to creating space for people and communities to lead. Learning from Fambul Tok and the Framework's success in Sierra Leone, they are now applying its lessons in Kenya, Guatemala, Afghanistan, Zimbabwe, Northern Ireland, the United States, and beyond.

When John and I first met in 2007, we couldn't have imagined most of what was to come. We only knew how we would start: by asking the communities in Sierra Leone what *they* wanted. By grounding in and continuing to true to our larger common vision and deeper purpose, we grew the program in practice, over time. That common vision and purpose called forth and enabled the kind of collaborative, creative, generative weaving work we did in Sierra Leone.

Ultimately, it's the vision of the larger whole—a healthy, regenerative, integral global community, held together by mutually liberatory relationships—that prompts, inspires, and undergirds my life's work. The vision of the whole I hold in my imagination is both *already* and *not yet*. It is true and present as something to turn to, to learn from, and to lean into, even while we work to bring it into clearer, visible expression around us. This whole is not imposed from the outside. It is not fragmented or fragmenting, not mechanical or mechanistic. It is alive and organic, unfolding and growing from within—if we let it.

Braiding peace

As someone trained in the system-as-it-has-been, I knew my ongoing learning and unlearning were critical. As Fambul Tok grew, I lived with the question: How do I need to transform myself in order to support the work we are doing?

That is not often a question that gets asked in the policy or training circles of peace and security, and certainly not among funders. But over and over, I saw that if I wanted to do and support work that could transform the world, I had to be willing to transform myself. And so, in this book as in my life, I weave together the story of our work in Sierra Leone and the story of the learning journey that enabled that work. Like a braid. Whenever I have been faced with things that seemed to be fragmented or in tension, I've seen an invitation to braid—to make a cord that is stronger for weaving together things that may appear different or even oppositional.

Which is exactly what I did when I encountered the firewall of separation between the world of the peacebuilding funder and that of the peacebuilding practitioner. I turned the tension I felt into an invitation to create a new kind of space, one where funding and practice work together in healthy relationship and as parts of the larger, healthy whole. I put the funds I received in an endowment and started my own granting and operating foundation, Catalyst for Peace (more on this in chapter 8). And I set about working to braid my sense of the world's need, my soul's deepest longings, and my commitment to transformative programming.

I firmly believe that the generation that makes the money should also experience the social good it can support, and so I knew I didn't want to create a perpetual endowment. I planned to spend down the funds and sunset the endowment over a generation—20 years, give or take. That time frame provided a spacious boundedness that has supported action and learning over time, step by step—strand by strand. It has supported a vision of my social change leadership as a creative practice, a kind of social poetry, allowing for an extraordinary interplay of artistry and productivity, imagination and activity.

Braiding the story

Braiding puts things in relationship to each other in a way that is both beautiful and functional, and in a way that makes the whole stronger than any part would be alone. We have done that in our work in Sierra Leone, I have done that with the different parts of my identity, and I do that now in this book.

In the coming chapters, I weave three strands together. The first is the story of Fambul Tok, both what it accomplished and how it worked. The second is the journey I had to make, as a person and as a leader, in order to work the way I wanted to. And the third is the framework supporting it all—the foundational convictions, the creative and spiritual practices, and the programmatic insights and approaches that supported transformation in Sierra Leone, and in me.

But this book is not any one of those strands exclusively or exhaustively. Rather, I aim to share enough of each for you to sense and savor the whole.

In part I, I share stories from the remote communities in Sierra Leone where Fambul Tok began its work and offer background about the history of Sierra Leone's civil war and of the international efforts to support peace. I also share John Caulker's story—his community roots, his harrowing wartime exploits as a human rights activist, and how he came to lead the call for reconciliation, believing in the power of his country's people, communities, and culture. I bring you to Fambul Tok's tradition-based reconciliation bonfires and cleansing ceremonies, and I share stories of the forgiveness and healing that came from them, including the transformation of a notorious wartime commander who became a leader for peace. I also walk you through the processes we used to make this work possible.

In part II, I share the story of how and why I came to this work, focusing on the resources that helped me challenge the norms of an international peace and security field dominated by secular, rational analysis. As I discover and learn to integrate previously untapped spiritual resources for peace, the separate threads of my spiritual life and my work in the world become increasingly interwoven. I show you how my peacebuilding work evolved and how I decided to use $20 million through Catalyst for Peace to help bring a new system to life. And I tell you about my encounter with northern Uganda's Acholi religious leaders, working to end the violence of the Lord's Resistance Army in their homeland. I share the insight from them that became foundational to my life's journey: What if existing international justice mechanisms were actually an obstacle to justice and peace? How can we instead live out a different system of accountability and community healing?

My journey and Fambul Tok's weave together in part III, "Building a Home for the Work," where I illuminate the key elements of our approach of "building peace from the inside out," showing what that has meant in practice. You'll learn how we structured our programming to support the nonlinear nature of real-world social change, including using action-reflection cycles and practicing "emergent design." You'll witness how we practiced storytelling *as* peacebuilding, not merely *about* peacebuilding, and how the relational, conversational skills of "hearing to speech" and "appreciative mirroring" illuminate important roles that outsiders can play.

My individual journey mirrored and supported the organizational journey. I share about how, at a critical moment in my own leadership, I had to humbly learn how to receive others' support, not just for the *work* but for *myself*, and how this led me to form my own Wisdom Circle. And I describe the metaphoric journey of "leaving my father's house," and how moving into a "home of my own" meant disentangling from a patriarchal, "outside-in" system.

In part IV, I describe how we had to adapt our programming and step into new levels of resilience and growth when Ebola struck Sierra Leone in 2014. You'll see the inadequacies of much of the international response up close, as well as the strength of the Fambul Tok model and the resilience it offered communities facing this new threat. You'll learn how we not only challenged the "business as usual" approach but also built, together with local leaders, a powerful alternative that opened the way for working differently.

In this part, I also drill down on two key metaphors at the heart of the theory behind our work. The first is the image of the community as a cup: a vessel that, when whole, can contain and support everything within it but, when cracked, can hold neither its own resources nor retain anything poured into it from the outside. This metaphor makes the community container visible and illuminates the necessary work of repairing the cracks, instead of simply pouring in aid and expecting that to "fix" problems. The second metaphor I introduce is the image of the international system as nested bowls—our vivid and powerful alternative to the linear, hierarchical assumptions of the status quo. This metaphor represents a whole-scale reconceptualization of the field and can inspire fundamental, necessary changes to the international system. These images, and the transformation they ask of leaders at every level, were crucial to bringing Fambul Tok's innovation to a national scale and, eventually, to it being adopted as government policy.

Part V unfolds the next step in Fambul Tok's evolution: the People's Planning Process, our community-based model for development, and its adoption as national policy through the Wan Fambul National Framework for Inclusive Governance and Local Development. I show how rural women's leadership in Sierra Leone was key to making that possible. I share how the Wan Fambul Framework was more than just a milestone accomplishment; it was inspirited by the vision of wholeness in community that grounded and resourced everything built to that point. And I complete the braid of the book: the individual journey that underpins my transformation and that of so many people on our journey; the journey of Fambul Tok's work, from the most remote villages of Sierra Leone to the national and international policy arenas; and the expression and invocation of wholeness, of the new, life-giving system, that can spring up when we work together from the inside out.

My story, this story, exists at the intersection of all the things you were told not to talk about in polite company: politics, money, and religion. I can't tell this story without bringing in each of those threads. It's not politics I write about, per se, but rather the systemic processes of social change, the transformation of the very way we think about organizing as a global community. It's not money I write about, per se, but rather aligning funding, relationships, programming, and values so that our financial resources enable us to call forward and live into our deepest shared values—together. And it's not religion I write about, per se, but rather the deeper spiritual ideas that inspire and support me and inform my work, and consequently the approach I have lived out more generally. The work of transformation is fundamentally spiritual, whatever that word may mean to you, and it is resourced by both the visible and invisible, the tangible and intangible.

As you journey through this book, there may be moments in which the balance of these threads feels surprising or uncomfortable to you. Where program detail seems too dense, feel free to skim, leaving us program nerds to exult in the complexity. As my personal learning journey unfolds, I invite you to look for yourself in the stories, too, whatever your life circumstances. If my candid discussions of spirituality touch an uncomfortable edge for you— welcome to the journey. I hope you will let it expand you.

Integration is not linear but circular and iterative. It happens in fits and starts, ebbs and flows, rhythms of expansion and contraction. I've tried to write with a rhythm that offers a path for your own iterative reflection and integration as you read. I encourage you to give yourself that space.

How I work is as important to me as what I do, and yet this is not a how-to book. It is a *how-I* book—how I have done what I've done and what I've learned in doing it. There are a lot of how-to implications from my experience and in the writing, but for the most part, they are meant to be an invitation, not a prescription. We are all in different places, physically and metaphorically. I invite you to let my stories spark self-reflection on your own deeper values, vision, purpose, and potential. I invite you to let these stories spark new possibilities and new imaginings in your own contexts. I invite you to look for that which you most want to see more of, and to find ways to come together with others to make more space for it in the world.

I invite you to find and hold to your own core, like in a French braid, and to find the people and possibilities to weave together with so that you, too, can bring your whole self as one part of a larger whole, where your self and the whole feed and sustain each other. My experience tells me that it's possible.

Holding fire

In the mid-2000s, I had the privilege of working with the Acholi Religious Leaders Peace Initiative (ARLPI), an extraordinary interfaith group of northern Ugandan religious leaders who came together to try to end the brutal civil war there, to end the reign of terror of the rebel Lord's Resistance Army, or LRA, and to help people and communities heal from the devastation and destruction. One of the founders, Anglican Bishop McLeod Ochola, became a hero of mine. Bishop Ochola's wife and daughter were both killed by rebels in the fighting that plagued northern Uganda, and yet he was leading national calls for forgiveness and a restorative justice process, even for those responsible for his own losses. He shared a beautiful metaphor for what helped and guided him in this process:

> Once the truth is known, it is very bitter for you to swallow. Truth is very deadly; it can kill. But how can you handle, accept it? It is only through mercy. Mercy can let you hold it. If you want to carry live fire in your hands, you will throw it away because it will burn. But if you hold it in something good, that does not conduct heat, you can take the fire. So it is the same with this, truth revealed—you can receive it with mercy.

You can handle the heat of painful truth by holding it in something good—something Bishop Ochola named as mercy. In Sierra Leone, we held the heat of truth with community. Fambul Tok has focused its work on repairing the fireproof container of community to hold the people and the work they and their country most need. A healing and whole community is itself a living organism.

Working *for* it helped people work *from* it—to live out the values and practices of a healthy and whole community in the present, even while working to grow its lived expression. A living whole greater than the sum of its parts, a restored community connects us to something bigger than ourselves, opening us to new inspiration, energy, and capacity. It is our channel to the universal, ancestral wisdom, at once invisible and yet so tangibly present and powerful that it can help us confront some of the most difficult challenges we face.

This greater wisdom, the wisdom of wholeness, is the ultimate fireproof container for the work we are called to do. I fundamentally believe that this wisdom wants to be more fully expressed in the world today. It wants to be expressed in us and to us, as individuals and as communities, and in and through the work we do. This greater wisdom feeds our core. It is the wholeness that ultimately holds us all. And it is a strong and trustworthy container.

Part I

HEALING AFTER WAR

Chapter 1

CROSSING OVER

March 2008

There is no bridge across the Manowa River. To get to the cluster of villages in Manowa section, a small region in Kailahun, the eastern-most district of Sierra Leone, you have to drive your vehicle onto a floating wooden platform, optimistically called a "ferry." The ferry is attached to a wire cable that straddles the river. Powered by two ferry "operators" pushing long poles, it slowly moves across the river. There's no use being impatient. There is simply no way to go any faster.

Even getting *to* the ferry takes spacious, gracious unconcern with time. That much I'd learned already, even though this was my first trip to Sierra Leone. To get this far, we'd left Freetown, the capital city on the edge of the Atlantic Ocean, the day before, and driven the length of the country, more than 11 hours through a panorama of open, gently rolling terrain. Unpaved road cut a curving, soft-red line through lush green fields. Scattered palm trees punctuated the blue sky like miniature green fireworks. As we got farther east, dark gray hills of volcanic soil framed the horizon. Red-caked leaves of roadside greenery boasted of the dry season's dusty gift to anything too close to the road. Even the air smelled dry.

In the best of times, Manowa would still be remote, but in post–civil war Sierra Leone, where roads destroyed in the war still hadn't been rebuilt or repaved, the journey felt like it moved in slow motion. Annual heavy rains deeply rutted the roads, some of which were more pothole than pathway, and navigating those by car could qualify as an Olympic sport. Fambul Tok's three-month-old Toyota Land Cruiser had already looked run-down and battered at the start of our journey, and now I understood why.

As the road wound through villages, I saw clusters of women with giant wooden mortars and pestles, rhythmically pounding rice to crack off its hard hulls. Bright-red palm kernels dried on tarps the size of family picnic blankets. Thatched-roof homes hugged the road. Once in a while, we'd see a zinc roof, often rusty, just like the NGO (nongovernmental organization) signs that littered the roadside, announcing who had helped whom do what in that place. The larger the town, the more signs clamoring for attention.

"Songo is that way," John Caulker said, pointing over the steering wheel as we crossed an early junction. John was the director of Fambul Tok, and Songo is where he grew up. As we drove, he shared memories of village life before the war destroyed his town, and of how hard it had been to resettle and rebuild after. He told stories of other places we drove by, too. He talked about the West Side Boys, a notorious gang active especially at the end of the war, as we passed their base at Okra Hills. Approaching Mile 91 (many places are commonly known simply by their distance from

Freetown), he pointed and said, "See that pile of rusted cars? This was called Foday Sankoh's Garage." Then he described how the rebels, under Foday Sankoh's command, would hide just over a hill and ambush vehicles when they reached the top, capturing everything and everyone and burning the cars.

At Mile 91, John gestured to his left and said casually, "That's where I would go to infiltrate rebel camps." As a young human rights advocate, he disguised himself as a rebel so that he could sit around their bonfire, listening as young fighters bragged about the day's events. Then he snuck out and looked for a phone to pass the information to his colleagues at Article 19 and Amnesty International.

It was a huge relief to spill out of the car and uncrumple my body when we finally stopped for the night. Exhausted from the day of driving, I was also filled with deep appreciation and even awe at the much longer life journeys that had brought John and his team to this place and this moment. We spent the night in Kailahun Town, the capital of Kailahun District. The town had once been a thriving hub of regional commerce, strategically located at the intersection of the Sierra Leone, Liberia, and Guinea borders. Then it became the place where the war began, and easily one of the country's most war-ravaged districts. The United Nations compound, which sometimes allowed internationals to rent rooms for the night, was the only secure place to stay in the district and, when the generators were running, the only place with regular electricity. But even the UN didn't have running water, and among the many things I learned on my way to Manowa was how to bucket flush.

The next morning, it was another two and a half hours, on the road and on the ferry, to reach Manowa. I was accompanying the Fambul Tok staff to Manowa's first gathering of community stakeholders, where John would ask if they wanted to engage with the *fambul tok* community reconciliation process. John never presumed he knew how the community wanted to approach reconciliation, and he paid special attention to consulting an inclusive group of traditional leaders, women, youth, elders, Muslims, Christians, victims, and perpetrators, explaining the *fambul tok* process and exploring whether and how they wanted to engage with it. The initial meeting was structured around a series of open-ended questions: Do you want to reconcile? If so, how? What resources do you have to begin that process? How can we walk with you and support you in the process? We trusted these were the right questions. But none of us knew exactly how the people of Manowa would answer them.

We went first to the section chief's house, and after the official greetings, we all walked together to the *court barray*, a covered, open-air community gathering space common in rural Sierra Leone. A large circle of chairs stretched to the edges of the *barray*. Stakeholders from all of the neighboring villages were beginning to gather, and the crowd grew so large that many people had to stand outside in the sun, where they nevertheless leaned in eagerly to be part of the conversation. As we talked together, it was immediately clear that no one in Manowa felt that they had experienced anything close to reconciliation, even though there had been a formal Truth and Reconciliation Commission (TRC) in the country. The TRC had comprehensively documented wartime atrocities and produced a multivolume report, but it had not offered space for people to reconcile with each other. There had been an unquestioned collective resignation to its impossibility, and communities had tried to move forward without it.

Yet when John asked the people of Manowa if they *wanted* to reconcile, there was a resounding, universal "Yes!" And when he asked them how they might like to do so, there was a visible awakening to the possibility. John explained that Fambul Tok valued Sierra Leone's cultural practices of communal truth-telling, apology, and forgiveness and recognized that communities had many other resources, already present within their villages, that they could use to lead their own reconciliation process. With that, the conversation grew loud and animated.

From the spillover crowd just outside the open sides of the *barray*, a tall gentleman came forward. Dressed all in white, with a white kufi cap that amplified his height and added to his air of distinction, he spoke deliberately, with an authority that immediately captured the crowd's attention. "No one's ever come here like this before," he said, expressing an almost stunned disbelief that we had traveled to Manowa at all, although clearly referring to more than the physical difficulties of actually getting there. "This is the first time we've ever been asked what *we* want."

He put our visit in the context of centuries of history, speaking like an excited schoolteacher lecturing on his favorite subject. "First the Christians came," he informed us, "and they said, 'Your culture is heathen. You need Christianity.' And then the Muslims came, and they said, 'No, no, your culture is bad, haram. You need Islam.' And then the colonizers came, and they said, 'No, no, your culture is backward. You need our civilization.'" His voice and his head dropped, and he added, "And then the war came and destroyed everything anyway."

With piercing directness he looked up at us. "You are the first people ever to come here and say, 'Your culture is valuable.' To believe that we have resources, ourselves, to address these challenges."

Now it was my turn to be stunned. I'd been hearing about this dynamic from John all along, of course. As the elder spoke, I recalled those rusted signs all along our drive. His words gave me a new understanding of how unconventional the ideas behind Fambul Tok gatherings really were: our presence, questions, and invitation; our deep listening and genuine commitment to "walking with," reinforced by walking so very far *to*, these villages—all of it countered decades, even centuries, of relationships with outsiders who had ignored, devalued, or destroyed what was there, imposing their own sense of what was valuable onto this community and ignoring its connections to its own ancestral wisdom. It wasn't only religious and colonial powers that had done so. Decades of humanitarian support had replicated the same dynamics, bringing outside "solutions" to "problems" that outsiders defined, without recognizing, much less engaging or mobilizing, the resources already in the community. The value of the local culture, of the talents, desires, experience, ingenuity, courage, commitment, knowledge, and caring relationships within the community itself—all of that had been left unacknowledged and uninvited.

Many others jumped in to echo the spirit of the elder's response, and after animated conversation, the community agreed unanimously to engage the *fambul tok* reconciliation process. Mere hours before, the crowd had said they didn't think reconciliation could ever happen. But simply being asked what they wanted, and what resources they might already have to facilitate that, had opened up a clear and immediate interest in working together to make it happen. That stakeholder meeting in Manowa inaugurated a three-month process in which Fambul Tok staff guided the villages of Manowa through organizing and running their own community healing bonfire.

The centerpiece of Fambul Tok was the *fambul tok* reconciliation process. (I denote the process in lowercase italics and the program we named after it using capitals.) The *fambul tok* process was designed over months of consultations with a wide range of local leaders across the country, and it centered around a two-day ceremony held in the community. On the first day, around an evening bonfire, people would tell stories of what happened to them during the war, or of what they had done, offering apologies and granting forgiveness to each other in front of the whole community. The ceremony revived the tradition of communal conversation and collective problem-solving and adapted it to help communities heal from the war. The next day, there would be a cleansing ceremony that revitalized traditional practices and reconnected communities with their ancestors—connections that had been dormant since the war, and sometimes even earlier, suppressed by the many phases of colonial interference the elder had described. The cleansing ceremony would be followed by months and ultimately years of community activities to deepen reconciliation, build on the relationships being rewoven, and address critical community needs with collective economic development projects.

The conversation in Manowa was only the first step in their long-term community healing process, and what happened there would be repeated with more than 2,500 villages, involving more than 150,000 people. But I'm getting ahead of myself.

Chapter 2

THE WAR AND THE PEACE

Sierra Leone's civil war began on March 23, 1991, when rebel leader Foday Sankoh ordered his Revolutionary United Front across the southeast border from Liberia, where it had enjoyed training and support from Charles Taylor's special forces. Sankoh wanted to overthrow the government, seated far on the other side of the country. The first blood in the 11-year war was spilled in the eastern border town of Bomaru, in Kailahun District, and the fighting quickly spread from there. By the war's end, more than fifty thousand people had been killed, and two million, one-third of the entire population, were displaced. The war razed whole communities and destroyed roads, bridges, schools, and hospitals. Amputation was a gruesomely common tool of terror, as machete-wielding fighters from all sides hacked off the arms, legs, fingers, toes, lips, or even noses of more than ten thousand people. More than ten thousand children were forced to take up weapons as child soldiers. Women were systematically targeted with sexual violence; an estimated quarter-million women and girls were raped, forced into "marriage," or subjected to other forms of sexual slavery and abuse.

When the war ended in 2002, the Sierra Leone government asked the United Nations to establish an international tribunal to prosecute war crimes and crimes against humanity. The Special Court for Sierra Leone was the first international tribunal since Nuremberg to sit in the country where the crimes took place, with satellite offices in The Hague and New York City. The Court indicted the thirteen people it deemed most responsible for the war and, over nine years, found nine of them guilty, including Liberia's Charles Taylor, the first African head of state to be convicted for his part in war crimes. Three others died in custody, and one of the indicted remains missing and is presumed dead. All told, the prosecutions cost, according to a senior United Nations official I spoke with, more than $500 million.

The peace accord ending the war also established a national Truth and Reconciliation Commission, which ran from 2002 to 2004. It aimed to provide another form of accountability for human rights abuses committed during the war, constructing a historical record of violations and promoting reconciliation. The TRC held public hearings in Freetown and in the capital cities of the other 12 districts. But the peace accord also granted amnesty to all but the war's senior leaders, giving most perpetrators of violence little incentive to testify during the TRC.

Rural Sierra Leoneans, who were the most affected by the war, generally had no way to attend these district hearings. With little or no access to motorized transportation, it can take several days for people from remote villages to reach their district capitals, and given the country's reliance on subsistence agriculture, few people had the time or resources to spend on such an effort. And even for those who could attend, the hearings themselves focused on official activities or closed-door meetings, leaving little time for public testimonies. In spite of its limitations, the TRC did produce a comprehensive account of atrocities in its 2004 report, a four-volume tome of more than five thousand pages.

Taken together, the two formal efforts toward justice and reconciliation had little impact on the day-to-day lives of most Sierra Leoneans, who perceived them as international efforts. They offered no path for ordinary people to achieve any measure of justice or begin the process of healing themselves and their communities. It was not uncommon for people to live next door to the person who had killed their father, amputated their arm, raped them or their mother, or burned down their house. Supported by government injunctions to "forgive and forget," no one talked about what had happened, much less reconciled. That made it virtually impossible to move forward—individually, communally, or nationally.

Fambul Tok was created to step into this void. It invited Sierra Leoneans to define justice in their own way, and it invited individuals to participate directly in their own reconciliation process—to whatever degree they wanted—alongside their communities. What I heard over and over again, in the hundreds of communities I visited over the years, was a vision of "justice" not as punishment of perpetrators—the line between victims and perpetrators in the war was thin and fluid—but rather as the work of making communities, and the people in them, whole again. That wholeness encompassed both victims *and* perpetrators, all of whom were seen as integral members of the community, the collective entity everyone wanted to see move forward and thrive.

Reclaiming the sacred

The first *fambul tok* bonfire happened on March 23, 2008, the 18th anniversary of the start of the war, in Bomaru, where the war had begun. By the time we arrived for the ceremony, Bomaru's place in the history of the war had been marked with a government-built monument in the middle of the town. The two-story, open-air tower drew attention and visits from dignitaries, but it was virtually ignored by the residents themselves, who had had little input in its construction. Children were already well-practiced in approaching visitors and inviting them to see the monument, but these invitations felt hollow, like the "locals" playing their part in someone else's scripted performance of commemoration.

Fambul Tok's consultative process offered a counterpoint to that approach and a kind of collective, communal identity formation in its own way. Fambul Tok had worked with the people of Bomaru for more than two months to plan their reconciliation bonfire and cleansing ceremony. By holding a space for communities to design, lead, and own the process, Fambul Tok was, in effect, holding the space for them to (re)create and (re)define not only justice but also their community itself.

So it felt all the more significant to me that the day of the first *fambul tok* bonfire also happened to be Easter Sunday. The *fambul tok* process did indeed signify a resurrection of sorts—of a community, yes, but also of an indigenous approach to justice and reconciliation. The process that made this resurrection possible was grounded in something both simple and profound: an assumption that the answers are there; that the communities, no matter how devastated, have the capacity to plan and lead a process that meets their own needs, as they see them. This was a foundational assumption in Fambul Tok's work, and it functioned like clearing the land before farming—helping remove the rocks and stumps and weeds that prevent new growth.

In Bomaru's case, there was also some literal land-clearing to be done before the bonfire. The community spent days clearing out the brush and removing overgrown trees and vines that hid their sacred rock, which stood just outside the town. The massive boulder had once been the site of sacred activities like communing with ancestors, but it had been neglected during the years of war and, before that, the decades of encounters with outside dogma that called traditional practices backward, useless, or even dangerous. In the planning conversations with Fambul Tok, the people of Bomaru saw an opportunity not just to make peace with each other by engaging in truth-telling around the traditional bonfire but to make peace with their ancestors, too, by engaging in ritual to return their sacred rock to its place of spiritual importance, and their community to right relationship with its traditions and cultural riches.

In Bomaru, the cleansing ceremony took place the morning after the bonfire. A long line of people walked the newly uncovered path, led by women of mixed ages who were singing and chanting along the way, many carrying *shekeres*, percussion instruments made from dried gourds strung with shells or beads. Younger residents, including some who had moved away but returned for the bonfire, exclaimed that they had never been to the rock before. Elders shared stories about ceremonial activity from years past and what it had meant to the people living there. The community had rekindled something that belonged uniquely to them, something that was at the core of their collective identity, and their pride was palpable.

John and I followed near the back of the line, excited to see what was going to unfold. We wanted to be unobtrusive, since we were there to honor the community's process, and to observe and learn, not to lead or interfere. When we reached the rock, we looked for a place on the edge of the crowd to sit and watch. Even with the area around the rock newly cleared, we were still in the middle of the bush; after an unexpected rain, it was a bit of a muddy mess. Undeterred, we scoped out a tree that we could sit under and lean against for what would no doubt be a long morning of watching and appreciating.

As we were sitting down, John motioned for me to wait. He stooped and took off his shoes and set them on the ground next to him, motioning for me to sit down on top of them. Instinctively, I started to refuse his offer, but I couldn't help but be touched by this unexpected gesture of care and concern, and I knew I needed to have the grace to receive it. With an appreciative smile, I sat down next to him to observe the ceremony, now (mostly) mud-free.

The ceremony was a reclamation, but also a modern adaptation. The community had decided, for example, that they wanted women to lead the way. Women in Bomaru and across the country had suffered uniquely during the war, targeted in particularly gruesome ways. As part of their healing, these same women had a deep desire to step into new leadership on behalf of their community. John and I would come to see that this was true for women across Sierra Leone.

The women who led our walk huddled together at one end of the rock as everyone else arrived. It was customary for the (male) chiefs to lead ceremonies and pour libations as an offering to the ancestors, but after everyone had gathered and before the chiefs came forward, the women spilled out from their corner and began singing and chanting and circling around and around the rock in a slow, rhythmic flow. There were old women and young women, many with babies on their backs, the bright and varied patterns of their clothes a symphony of color.

Around and around they circled and sang, as if gently but joyfully awakening the rock and reclaiming it for themselves and their community. They were sanctifying a new-old heart-center, and they were doing it in a new way—with music and movement, with young babies and old souls, with, and as, women. They were living witnesses to, and agents of, their own and their community's wholeness, even in the middle of brokenness and the in-process-ness of renewal. The circle of women didn't just reclaim the rock; they reclaimed the space of spirit—the spirit of the community.

Chapter 3

THE PARTNERSHIP

John and I had met only six months before we sat by Bomaru's sacred rock, but the journeys that led us to each other had begun long before. The youngest of six children, John grew up in the rural village of Songo, about 30 miles from Freetown, the nation's capital. His father left when John was very young, and his mother, Annie Caulker, a woman of deep faith and even deeper determination, raised her six children mostly on her own. Her encouragement to courageous action, commitment, and companionship with God shaped John's life. Whenever he faced a challenge, she told him, "Go try, ya. God be with you." Sometimes John succeeded; sometimes he failed. But he could always count on his mother's faith in him.

So could many other children. Annie was a teacher and the headmistress of the primary school in Songo, and she went out of her way to do anything and everything she could to make sure that every child she knew got a good education. She accepted everyone who wanted to go to school, even if they couldn't afford the fees or the uniforms. If they had nowhere nearby to stay, they stayed with Annie and John and the older siblings still at home. Whenever she cooked a meal, Annie sent John to take food to families who didn't have any, even if it meant they went a little hungry themselves sometimes. When John asked his mother why she took care of so many *other* people's children, she told him she thought of every child as her child, and that she hoped others would do the same if her children were ever in need.

In 1993, John began his studies at Freetown Technical Institute. The war in Sierra Leone had begun two years earlier, in the east of the country, but the fighting was slow to reach the capital. As a student, John became an activist against rising tuition fees, and soon he was leading the National Union of Sierra Leone Students, organizing a nationwide student strike that was averted at the last minute when he negotiated a fee reduction agreement. It was his first experience of activism, and it emboldened him to continue to raise issues and especially to advocate for the poor.

In 1995, four years into the war and while John was at university, the rebels reached Songo. Annie was forced to leave everything behind and flee with two children who were staying with her at the time. She escaped just in time; the rebels destroyed the whole village, including their family home, and anyone remaining was captured or killed. Even the dogs were killed. Annie fled to her family in Freetown, but they didn't welcome her as she'd hoped. The war still hadn't reached the capital, and her family didn't believe her story. They accused her of making up excuses so that she didn't have to work, and after only a couple of months, they kicked her out.

Annie took the two children to live with one of her daughters—six people in just one room. John visited regularly, and she often told him that she felt her voice was not heard, whether by society or by her own family, because she was poor.

A year and a half later, when he knew the rebels had left Songo, John took his mother and the children back home. They were the first to return. When others heard that "Mrs. Caulker was back in Songo," they felt safe enough to move back too. But the village had been devastated, and life was hard for everyone. Annie and John lived off meager money from selling mangoes and palm kernels from their land as they tried to rebuild their house. John felt the whole village's struggle, but he also saw people helping each other, even if they were hardly able to survive themselves. Some of the families his mother had once helped gave them food when they most needed it. The community came through, even when their biological family hadn't.

As the war progressed, John became a human rights researcher for organizations like Amnesty International. He sent them reports of what was happening on the ground, and they issued press statements to the world, careful never to name him or their other informers. After a few years, he began to question why only outsiders spoke about what was happening in Sierra Leone. "Why can't we have Sierra Leoneans speaking for ourselves, on our own behalf?" he asked his mother. He told her he wanted to start his own human rights organization; he wanted the voices speaking for his country to come from the inside. Though many others told him he was crazy, she supported him. "Go try, ya. God be with you," she said.

And so, in 1996, John founded Forum of Conscience to educate his fellow citizens about their rights and responsibilities, and to speak the truth of what was happening in Sierra Leone, especially in its rural areas, on a national and global stage. Crisscrossing the country, he saw up close how rural disenfranchisement led people into the fighting that was engulfing the country. He conducted human rights workshops in camps for people displaced by the conflict, and he continued to sneak into rebel camps. In both places, he repeatedly saw how people on both sides of the fighting—those committing atrocities and those hurt by them—were just ordinary human beings. When he approached them as people, not perpetrators or victims, all were eager to talk. He realized that this was going to be the only way to discover the truth about what had happened during the war: through conversation, in community.

Then his mother fell ill, and not long after, she died. John blamed the war, because all the doctors had fled the country, and her family, because they had forced her to endure so much hardship. It wore her out, and she died in Freetown only a few days after going there to seek medical care. Hers was the last burial in the city as new fighting erupted in 1998, when a regional peacekeeping force began a campaign to topple the military junta. Her wake was interrupted twice by gunshots. While everyone fled the church, John hid under her casket, unwilling to abandon his mother. He wrote her a note and placed it inside her casket: "Go try, ya. And God go with you."

John doubled down on his activism. He was an equal opportunity gadfly, calling out every injustice, regardless of affiliation—government or rebel, national or international. After he criticized the junta government on a Voice of America radio program, a group of thugs came to arrest him in his office. He escaped only by pretending to be someone else, badmouthing "that foolish man John Caulker" and promising to call them when Caulker showed up. He went underground after that, until the junta was out of power again.

As the peace efforts began to get serious, John became one of the first Sierra Leoneans to advocate for the Truth and Reconciliation Commission. He wanted "justice" included in the name as well, and he wanted the Commission to link amnesty to truth-telling. Otherwise, he thought, what incentive would anyone have to give a full account of wartime atrocities? Yet in the end, amnesty was given to all but the most senior leaders—regardless of whether they participated in the truth-telling.

John shifted his focus to advocating for meaningful local involvement in the Commission, and he worked tirelessly as the head of the TRC Working Group, a coalition of more than 40 local and national organizations that made up the civil society arm of the Commission. He advocated at every turn for full community engagement in the planning process, and he wanted to see smaller, localized proceedings in which anybody who wanted could participate. "It's never been done that way," everyone kept telling him, dismissing the idea. But he was determined—and unapologetic.

In early 2000, John spent three months in Geneva on a human rights fellowship, just as the Sierra Leonean parliament authorized the Truth and Reconciliation Commission. John worried that the government was not committed to ensuring its reach in rural areas. While he was in Geneva, he wanted to meet with the Office of the High Commissioner on Human Rights (OHCHR), which was managing the TRC process, to advocate for mobilizing strong involvement at the most local levels. His requests to meet were ignored or rebuffed, so he issued a press release criticizing the

TRC's lack of engagement with local leadership. Without better effort, he warned, the TRC would be seen by Sierra Leoneans as "something imposed from the outside."

John also called for the Sierra Leonean government to relieve the OHCHR of its responsibilities in running the TRC process. Suddenly, the OHCHR had time for him. In a frantic phone call, a senior official called John a "small boy" and asked him, in a tone simultaneously scolding and threatening, "Do you know what you've done? What damage you've caused?" After he returned home, the UN tried to remove him as chair of the TRC Working Group. But they failed: John had such strong relationships from all his work in the districts, and the very leaders for whom he'd been advocating refused to allow his removal. "They weren't able to get rid of me because my constituency was nationwide," he told me later. Once again, when others abdicated their responsibilities and tried to malign John for their own failures, his community stood by him and protected him.

The Ford Foundation offered John a grant in support of his vision for the TRC, and he used it to extend his networks across the country to lay the foundation for a more localized reconciliation process. When that funding ran out, the TRC still hadn't reached rural communities—places John knew had not only been the most ravaged by the war but also held powerful resources for peace. By the time the TRC finished its work, John had the beginnings of a national community-mobilizing infrastructure—but no capacity to build on it from there.

So when Sara Terry, a documentary photographer gathering stories about reconciliation and forgiveness after the war, walked into John's Freetown office one August day in 2007, she found him exhausted and discouraged, quite nearly convinced there would never be a chance for people in his country to really reconcile.

John told Sara about his vision for locally led reconciliation, and his thwarted efforts at supporting it in any systemic way. Sara, who was working with me on the storytelling project, immediately sensed how in sync his vision was with mine. "I know someone you have to meet!" she told him.

At the time, I was five years into running Catalyst for Peace, the private granting and operating foundation I had founded in 2003. I believed ordinary people were the great untapped resource in international peace and development, and I wanted to use Catalyst's resources to create peacebuilding opportunities that put people in the center and in charge. I wanted the communities most affected by war and violence to take the lead in building their peace. And I wanted to share the stories of this work with the world, to magnify its impact. I knew of many worthy peacebuilding initiatives that were grounded at the local or community level, but I also saw that these were mostly isolated and episodic. I wanted to help make that work more strategic and systemic, and to help the world learn how to work that way.

In a wink from synchronicity, John was scheduled to come to the US on a human rights fellowship at Columbia University two weeks after meeting Sara. I invited him to come to my office in Maine for a day so that we could get to know each other and begin exploring what might be needed and possible in Sierra Leone, as well as how our interests and capacities might align in addressing those needs and possibilities.

I also invited my friend and colleague Amy Potter (later Czajkowski) to join us, to be another set of eyes and ears in exploring a potential partnership. Amy, who had been a student of mine when I was a political science professor at Principia College, now worked at Eastern Mennonite University's Center for Justice and Peacebuilding, where she had a colleague who had worked with John during his TRC days. That connection, along with her ability to hold expectant, open space for new possibility, helped put John (and me) at ease as we began our conversation.

I was excited about the possibilities with John, and I was nervous. So much was unknown and uncertain, and the conversation held an implication that Catalyst for Peace might fund some of his work in Sierra Leone, which raised the stakes considerably. Money issues are fraught in general, and money issues involving white Americans and black Africans exponentially more so. I also knew that in addition to whatever funding Catalyst might provide, I would want to be actively involved *as a partner* in whatever work might emerge from our conversations, and I knew moving in that direction would require a high level of trust from John. Of course, I was listening for how much of my own trust to offer as well, but perhaps surprisingly, my anxiety was more focused on how I would earn *his* trust.

John flew up from New York for the day, and Amy and I met him at the airport. He was easy to spot, coming to the whitest state in the US (another fact that made me self-conscious). We exchanged warm but nervous greetings, and he put his backpack in my trunk. Then laughter broke the tension: We had the same exact backpack. Our sturdy blue JanSports sat side by side, impossible to tell apart.

We drove to my office, located in a repurposed historic movie theater in downtown Portland, and we spent most of the day there, talking. I was trying to act informal and help him feel comfortable while also clearly holding parts of myself in reserve—as was John, but even more so. Outwardly friendly, he nevertheless sat stiffly, literally on the edge of his seat, and he spoke and moved cautiously. We shared tea on that early fall day, which was just cool enough to justify wrapping my hands around the mug, and I appreciated having something to do with them rather than having to keep them folded stiffly in my lap. It felt gracious to have a whole day together to talk, which allowed our stories about ourselves and our peacebuilding journeys to unwind and circle back naturally over the course of the day, each time with more depth and comfort. By the afternoon, we had both settled back into our comfy chairs.

John shared about Sierra Leone's tradition of evening bonfires and explained more about the culture of forgiveness and the centrality of community to accountability and healing. He described the work he had already done in all 12 rural districts to lay the foundation for a local, accessible reconciliation process. His groundwork had confirmed his vision that a local process was both desired and possible, and it meant he already had networks in each district that he could mobilize to help begin this process across the nation.

Meanwhile, I spoke of my core convictions and motivating vision, and of the work I had been doing in northern Uganda, the Philippines, and southern India that had helped shape and confirm that vision. I spoke about my faith in ordinary people and my commitment to working in a way that created a space for people as people to be engaged directly in their own peace processes. I tried to describe my central animating desire to find ways to run people-centered programs at a systemic scale—to learn in practice what it would mean to do that work in a strategic way. And I tried to convey how deeply I believed that the answers are there—that even in the places most decimated by war, poverty, or other challenges, the people and communities themselves have answers and resources to address those challenges. I explained the roots of those convictions in my faith upbringing and my academic studies, and I told John about my conversations with northern Ugandan Acholi religious leaders, who opened my eyes to the ways in which the international justice system could fundamentally undermine local resources for peace.

Still, I felt woefully inadequate at conveying how genuine and embodied my values were, and that I could be a true, reliable partner in grounding a program in them. Even as I spoke, I worried that it all just sounded like words—abstract words, at that—especially next to John's concrete and contextualized vision and experience.

Somehow, we wended our way to imagining together what a nationwide community-centered reconciliation program in Sierra Leone might look like and how it might begin to come together. Meanwhile, Amy's strong program-building lens helped us imagine a concrete way forward. What would it actually take to create a community-centered process in Sierra Leone that valued and drew on its culture and traditions? And what would it take to support such a process to grow it to a national scale? John envisioned ceremonies held directly in impacted communities so that people could face those they had wronged or those who had wronged them and acknowledge, apologize, and forgive—in front of their communities. That, he believed, would enable the communities as a whole to move forward together. He expressed such a strong, natural, and infectious belief in what the people of his country could do given a process that invited and supported their leadership.

By the end of the day, it was clear to me how fully in sync our visions and values were, in addition to our backpacks. Yes, I had learned more about John's experience, networks, and organizational capacity—all critical resources he would bring to any work we might do together—and that helped me feel ready to move forward in partnership. But I also sensed at a deep level how fully aligned we were, not just in what we wanted to do but in what we believed to be possible, and in *how* we most yearned to work in service of turning that possibility into reality. That feeling of alignment is what contributed most significantly to building trust for me. I knew instinctively that our relationship would be a key component of any work we would do together, though I would come to learn much more over the next decade about the full scope of what that would mean and require. Nevertheless, after our day together, I had a strong sense that with such clear commonality of vision and values and a shared commitment to living them out in practice, everything else would take care of itself.

Toward the end of our time together, John finally shared a fear. Slowly and softly, he repeated what he'd heard so often from others: "It's never been done this way before . . ." I leaned in and rubbed my hands together. "Good! Why would we want to do something that's already been done?!"

Two months later, we'd signed our first grant agreement for Fambul Tok, and John was headed home to start the work.

Chapter 4

COMMUNITY HEALING

The afternoon melted into early evening in Daabu, a tiny village in a remote part of Kailahun District. A rebel stronghold during the war, Daabu had been the site of many atrocities. Seven years later, it still bore physical and psychic scars. Daabu's *court barray* was once a thriving community center, but it had been burned down during the war. Its charred remains were a visual reminder of the division and disconnection that now paralyzed the community. Its ruins, with weeds growing in the cracks, literally and metaphorically dominated the center of the village. It was a gaping wound, left alone and untended.

Until now.

A lone drummer began a soft but insistent beat; the sound called people to gather. Other musicians joined in, and people steadily arrived, gathering in an open dirt clearing next to the burnt-out *barray*. Children danced, carefully avoiding the massive pyramid of dried branches and gathered wood that sat in the middle of the clearing. The spontaneous drumming and dancing turned more purposeful, both calling and celebrating—celebrating everyone's presence and their shared purpose. People sat on rocks, chairs, benches, anything they could find. As darkness fell, village leaders reached torches into the tower of wood until it burst into flames. As the fire settled into a steady burn, the crowd also settled into its own alert, alive, almost quiet circle.

The bonfire crackled; sparks shot into the air in a display of natural micropyrotechnics. Rain clouds threatened, but the energy was electric. People were here not only because they wanted to participate but also because they wanted to see what would happen. They seemed committed but also measured and even anxious. Leaning in, yet wary and watchful.

It was March of 2009, just over a year into the Fambul Tok program and four months into Daabu's planning process, when its residents joined people from neighboring villages for their *fambul tok* reconciliation bonfire. I sat behind the crowd, feeling both eager and uncertain.

Sitting among the crowd was Chief Maada Alpha Ndolleh, tall even when seated, with an easy smile. He was middle-aged but looked youthful, wearing jeans, an untucked black cotton football jersey, and a well-worn yet gleaming-white baseball cap with the Fambul Tok logo. Originally from Daabu, he was the town chief of Kailahun Town, the capital of the district, and the chairman of the Fambul Tok district committee. In that role, Chief Ndolleh moved from village to village with the Fambul Tok staff, opening honest conversations about the war and laying the groundwork for reconciliation. He traveled thousands of miles and devoted thousands of hours to helping Fambul Tok succeed in his district's 14 chiefdoms, home to more than half a million people. And he did it all on a volunteer basis. As he crisscrossed the district, he saw people's initial hesitation about coming forward to testify. They hadn't seen anything like this since the war, and they were afraid. They didn't know what the exposure of their stories might mean. "They were thinking about the Special Court, thinking about a witch hunt," he told me later.

Chief Ndolleh stood and was preparing to address the crowd when a woman approached him. She seemed especially nervous. Before the bonfire began, she wanted to know, from the leader's own mouth, that she could accuse even a powerful person of committing a wrong against her. Chief Ndolleh affirmed this. "Talk about what happened to you during the war," he encouraged her. "If you don't explain, whenever you are passing a perpetrator, you will get that fear in your mind. If you explain, you will feel free."

Then the chief walked to the middle of the circle, next to the bonfire, and welcomed the crowd. He reminded them why they were gathered, and how they could finally talk about what had happened in this place during the war. He urged people not to be afraid to speak, emphasizing that those who confessed would not be prosecuted, nor would there be any shame for those who shared how they had been hurt. "If something is disturbing you, you have to speak it out," he said passionately. "And when you speak it out, you'll be relieved. You can once again talk with your brothers and sisters." Chief Ndolleh described similar bonfires across the district where people found great relief in telling their stories, in apologizing, and in offering or receiving forgiveness.

Hardly able to wait for the introductions to finish, a young man jumped up and walked purposefully into the center of the circle, near the fire. He faced his community with eagerness and resolve. His name was Michael Momoh, and he described the day the rebels first came into Daabu, capturing him and ordering him to find them food. As they roamed the area, they found a family working on their farm. The family fled, all escaping except their seven-year-old daughter, who was captured. The rebels ordered Michael to tie her up and beat her, which, in shock himself, he did. He beat her so badly that she later died.

"I need peace, and I want my conscience to be clear," he said with intention and intensity. "I am confessing so that they forgive me. It was not my wish; I was under duress. I did not do it out of my own wish."

"Is the mother of the child here?" the elder facilitating the ceremony asked. With hardly a minute to process what Michael had just confessed, Mariama Jumu came forward, acknowledging that it was her daughter whom Michael had killed that day. Michael approached her and leaned over in a deep bow, a cultural symbol of repentance and submission. With the whole community watching, he begged Mariama to forgive him for what he had done. She touched his bowed head, a symbol of her acceptance of his apology, and said, "Yes." They embraced and danced together as their neighbors watched and clapped; then everyone joined in the dancing and singing.

It was a stunning moment on many levels. That a perpetrator had jumped forward to initiate the truth-telling and apology. That Mariama was so quick to accept his apology and express her forgiveness. That right away they could embrace and dance together, embodying their commitment to a new future—side by side, ready to go forward together.

People testified in a constant stream that night, sharing stories of their experiences during the war. Their earlier fear disappeared; they were propelled by an eagerness to move forward, by the desire to reconcile, to talk about what happened with their community. By the will to acknowledge, apologize, and forgive . . . together.

The next day, I discovered that Michael and Mariama lived literally next door to each other in this tiny village. And they told us that *they had never spoken of what had happened.* Not to each other, and not to anyone else. Prior to the ceremony, Mariama had avoided Michael completely. If he was part of an activity, she wouldn't join. If there was a meeting he was attending, she wouldn't go. As neighbors in the intimate circle of thatched-roof mud houses that make up the village of Daabu, they lived in isolation—from each other and from the community itself. And they were not the only ones. This pattern repeated itself across the village and in other villages across the country. This is the invisible nature of broken community: where webs of connection have been severed, it's almost impossible for anyone, much less the community as a whole, to go forward, to develop.

Catalyst for Peace was filming a documentary about Fambul Tok. After the bonfire, Sara interviewed Mariama about her daughter and what happened during the war in general. Mariama spoke of the sadness she carried about her child's death, but she nonetheless reiterated her forgiveness in a very straightforward way: Because Michael had confessed, she forgave him. She felt that forgiveness was important, in her words, "for unity and progress. For us to live together. For our community to forge ahead in terms of development. If we are not together, for us to work, it would be very difficult."

Mariama's answer is consistent with what we heard so many others say after they, too, offered forgiveness to someone who had harmed them. The speed of the forgiveness is beyond most Westerners' comprehension, and when they hear about it, a common response is disbelief.

"Did someone *tell* you to think this way?" Sara asked Mariama. "Or do you actually feel this inside your heart?"

Mariama looked slightly annoyed when the question was translated for her. But she nodded calmly, then quietly straightened and settled back on her bench. "Well, we are able to think for ourselves on these things," she said bluntly. "Once we've come together, we are going to continue."

Hers was a powerful and deceptively simple statement. But it's astonishing how rarely the people of Sierra Leone have felt that those coming to help them—whether to build peace, to support economic development, or to address other problems—demonstrate a real belief in their ability to think for themselves. Yet I have seen so much transformational energy come alive in communities when their members feel that their agency and capacity are respected and valued. When the community members' resources—their knowledge and desires and energy and talents—are recognized; when they are invited to *lead*; when outsiders come not merely as experts but as *learners*, eager to work in support of and alongside local leadership—when that happens, I have seen people in communities across Sierra Leone step forward with incredible energy and commitment and capacity.

At Catalyst for Peace, we call this an *inside-out* approach to peacebuilding and development—where the people "inside," who are closest to the issues being addressed, lead in the work of addressing them, and those "outside" the locality hold the space for that leadership, inviting and accompanying and supporting its growth and development. Our experience in Sierra Leone showed me that this way of working is not the norm in peacebuilding and development, and that countering the ingrained patterns and expectations of decades of outside-in work requires a great deal of attention and energy, especially when working at scale, as we were. But the result is that communities experience the program as both grounded in their wisdom and explicitly designed to build from their wisdom in its implementation. And that brings about not only profound transformation but also change that lasts and continues to ripple out.

Community—a living entity

Michael and Mariama's story shows what can happen when people feel reconnected to their ancestral, communal wisdom. Now they interact regularly; Michael calls Mariama "Ma," and she refers to him as a son. He carries water for her, helps with her farming, and does other household chores when she needs it, wanting to make up as much as he can for the absence of the child who would have grown to support her mother and the family. They also work side by side on community initiatives, alongside others in Daabu who used to avoid each other at all costs.

Their story also exemplifies the way the community itself holds a healing presence and power for reconciliation. Michael didn't approach Mariama in the privacy of her home. Living next door to her, he no doubt would have had ample opportunity. Rather, he opened up to tell his story in front of his whole community, and even several neighboring villages. In Sierra Leonean culture, the presence of the community is crucial to the forgiveness process. Acknowledgment of and apology for a wrong must happen *in front of the community* before forgiveness can be considered. Why? What Sierra Leoneans describe as the "naming and shaming" that occurs in this context is felt to be fitting punishment, even more severe than being sent to jail in most instances. Given the central value the culture places on connection of the individual to and through community, and especially on contributing *to* that community, this makes sense. As Fambul Tok national staff member Tamba Kamanda noted, "Without your community, you are nothing."

In Sierra Leone, as in much of Africa and across many indigenous cultures, the community is more than just an aggregation of individuals. It is a living entity with the responsibility to care for all the individuals who are part of it. Mariama had been carrying the burden of her daughter's death by herself. Alone. That made it almost unbearable. But after telling her story, and having it heard by the community, she felt the whole community helping her to carry that burden. Like Bishop Ochola's fireproof container for difficult truths, a healthy and connected community helped Mariama hold her pain. Though it doesn't bring her daughter back, it does lighten her load significantly. And it also restores her dignity, as well as Michael's.

Bringing her story to the community through the bonfire ceremony meant that Mariama could count on her neighbors to support her in future challenges, including the ongoing sadness she might wrestle with around the loss of her daughter. She could reliably trust that the witness of her community members would help ensure that Michael would not hurt her or her family again. As witnesses, they became, in essence, obligated as custodians—of her security and of her story. From the perspective of someone seated at that bonfire, this healed and healing community was a living body, with its own power and agency; in more social science-y language, it would be a felt network of connections and concrete relationships. This embodied relational mutuality and interconnection would be understood as a concrete, tangible resource to each person there. Knowing and anticipating that communal support helped Mariama accept Michael's apology and offer her forgiveness—she was willing to give something in advance of it being earned, knowing that she, too, would be receiving support from her community in advance of it being offered. Prevenient grace for all.

The Daabu bonfire, including its monthslong preparation process, helped revitalize the community as the living body that held all of its members so that it could be present in spirit and in action for Mariama and Michael, and many others, as they initiated their reconciliation. The ceremony itself also helped forward Daabu's community (re)formation process more directly. Put another way, the ceremony both signaled and served community healing.

Leaders too . . .

The *fambul tok* process demanded a lot of its leaders, but it also enabled them to accomplish a lot. Fambul Tok marked good leaders not by how much attention they drew to themselves but rather by how fully they worked for the betterment of their whole community, embracing the personal sacrifice that goal often required.

In Fambul Tok's rubric, the best leaders were those who made the most space for *others'* growth and development—for others' leadership. This was a new vision of leadership, one that both demanded and enabled a lot for individuals and for the whole country, where "Big Man" notions of leadership still dominated.

Daabu's bonfire offered powerful examples of new leadership in action. When a former rebel commander named Gabriel Ngegba came forward, his story tested the community's willingness to forgive. Gabriel told how he had been ordered by his commander to attack Daabu and destroy its *court barray*, and he in turn passed that command on to his troops, who carried it out. Because the *barray* is the social and commercial center of a Sierra Leonean village, burning it down was an assault on the whole community. It was the first time the people of Daabu learned who was responsible for that destruction.

In a case like this, where the victim is the collective, the chief would be vested with responding on the community's behalf. But the local town chief, Chief Ganawa, was so angry after hearing the story that he jumped up and ran at Gabriel, yelling and hitting him. A fight broke out as others joined in. The bonfire had to be paused to break up the fight and make space for the town to decide what it wanted to do. As the chair of Fambul Tok's organizing committee in Kailahun, Chief Ndolleh helped facilitate the conversation. In the vigorous discussion that ensued, many villagers begged Chief Ganawa to forgive Gabriel so that the community could move forward. Although personally reluctant, the chief accepted his community's wishes. "I don't have any alternative," he said when the bonfire resumed and he stood in the center of the circle to speak to the crowd. "My people have spoken to me. And for the development and peace, I have forgiven him." Chief Ganawa had allowed the community, in essence, to lead *him*—from indignation and reprisal to forgiveness and collective repair.

Chief Ganawa wasn't the only leader sublimating personal feelings on behalf of his community. Chief Ndolleh's work throughout the district exemplified an extraordinary model of leadership as sacrificial commitment to the community's welfare. And the Daabu bonfire proved a new and very personal testing ground for him.

In Sierra Leone, chiefs represent an older, more traditional, more trusted leadership system, and their approval is crucial for initiatives, especially those that come from outside the village. Because Kailahun was so affected by the war, only someone with Chief Ndolleh's stature could have opened the way for a process like Fambul Tok's to move forward. Little did he know that he would be called upon to trust in the *fambul tok* process himself.

At the bonfire, the woman who'd asked Chief Ndolleh for permission to accuse a powerful person came forward to accuse . . . him. She said that he had stolen her family's meat during the war and ordered people to beat her husband. Her testimony surprised him, and the community. Many people urged the chief not to step forward to respond. As chief, they said, he didn't have to answer to such people, or for such things. Yet Chief Ndolleh stood up and went into the center of the circle, where he apologized and accepted responsibility for what he had done. After describing how hard things were at that moment in the war, Chief Ndolleh acknowledged he had given the order to take the food. "If what I did did not go down well with you, I'm asking you to forgive me," he concluded. His accuser acknowledged his remarks as an apology and offered him forgiveness. Arm in arm, they walked out of the circle together.

To many listeners, Chief Ndolleh's words hardly constitute a perfect apology, or perhaps even much of an apology at all. Rarely do these encounters sound as outsiders might expect them to. But even imperfect words carry important meaning to those they are meant for. Context, too, carries incredible significance. For a chief to own up to something he did—in public, before a huge gathering of the people he leads—was itself extraordinary, and coming forward after the woman accused him sent a strong, singular message.

The moment was a critical embodiment of the power and safety of the *fambul tok* space. In any other circumstance, it would have been unthinkable for someone, especially a woman, to call out a chief in public for *anything*. In fact, John told me afterward, "If it was done outside of that bonfire space, it would have been a crime." But Chief Ndolleh was committed to modeling the values of the program, values he had worked so hard to spread across his district, and he knew he had to publicly accept responsibility. He allowed the process and values to pull him away from the exalted separateness of chiefs and into direct personal engagement and communal accountability, just like everyone else. Chief Ndolleh had allowed the process and values to lead him. As a nationally visible leader in the *fambul tok* process, he set an example that opened the way for people everywhere to talk about what their chiefs did during the war.

Both chiefs' examples modeled an extraordinary commitment to leading by serving what is good *for the whole*, and to using their positions to make space for others' voices, especially those not often heard. When leaders live out the values they advocate, their examples can magnify transformation. When a program is structured to invite and support that, what is good for the whole can truly . . . lead.

Chapter 5

THE CONTAINER FOR RECONCILIATION

Even though Fambul Tok based its work on Sierra Leonean cultural notions of justice, which center around the restoration of individual and communal wholeness, John knew that the *fambul tok* process would only be trusted and effective if it was both local and locally owned. "Local ownership" has become a buzzword and, like so many buzzwords, is much easier to say than to imagine in concrete terms, let alone to build in practice. John and I embedded our commitment to local ownership in every stage of our work, both in principle and in process, framing our role around the ideas of accompaniment. While we worked hard, in pathbreaking ways, to anchor this work locally, we simultaneously held a vision for facilitating healing on a national scale—for creating the process and infrastructure that would support hundreds of communities across the country.

To do this, we grounded both programming and process in a simple but often overlooked truth: In Sierra Leone, the community is not simply the place where people live, or an aggregation of individual people. It is a living entity in and of itself. It is a presence. It has power. It shapes people's identities in fundamental ways. And this entity was also ripped apart and destroyed in the war, along with people and property. In designing Fambul Tok's community-centered approach, we made choices big and small that focused on helping communities reweave the social fabric and repair the container that held their community together as a whole, even in the middle of hardships and brokenness. And when that happened, we saw how the people and community could really heal themselves.

We grounded every iteration of *fambul tok* in a thorough community consultation process, like the one in Manowa. These consultations were not the usual perfunctory gatherings of a few senior-level, mostly male leaders—the kind of meetings that tick the box to show you've "consulted" the people before you go ahead and do what you had intended to do all along. Nor were they singular events; rather, they were structured as an ongoing process. In Fambul Tok's approach, consultations were serious investments of resources—especially of time and relationship-building offered by the Fambul Tok staff. And these investments impacted program design. For example, staff initially envisioned holding ceremonies at the chiefdom level (analogous to the county level in the US), but communities felt that these ceremonies needed to be even more locally based to enable full access and participation. So Fambul Tok redesigned the program and planned for ceremonies at the sectional level (a grouping of anywhere from five to fifteen villages). And when communities expressed the desire to revive long-neglected traditions of ceremonial cleansing and communing with ancestors specifically to address the lingering wounds of the war, the cleansing ceremony became a core part of the *fambul tok* reconciliation process. Consultations were thus built in as a programmatic element (process *as* program), but even more importantly, they themselves also shaped our emerging program design.

Even once the overall *fambul tok* process was established, local communities had full ownership of the planning process for their individual ceremonies. Each cleansing ceremony, for example, was organized by the communities hosting it, according to their unique traditions and wishes, which varied by location. Some villages with stronger connections to a church or mosque preferred to undertake sacred rituals in their houses of worship, and they would choose to perform their cleansing ceremony in that space. Others chose to congregate at sacred ancestral sites or town centers. In any case, the main idea was that it was up to the communities themselves to choose, and Fambul Tok adapted its program design accordingly.

Unlike most typical humanitarian aid organizations in Sierra Leone, Fambul Tok never planned programming from outside and brought it to "target communities" only for implementation. A core Fambul Tok value is to *go to* and *walk with* communities during the planning and implementing of a program they build as their *own*. This is what we mean when we say that the *fambul tok* process is "community owned and led." By the same token, it exemplifies that the critical role for outsiders—whether they are from half a world away or even from the same country or district—is to support and maintain the space for *that community's ownership* to develop. "Going to" and "walking with" are enabling roles, part of the overall approach I describe as *accompaniment*.

The accompaniment process—the real work of creating space for local ownership—does not happen quickly. The bonfire testimonies were only possible because of months of dedicated, detailed, deliberate preparatory work by Fambul Tok staff and volunteers in each section and village. Fambul Tok began working in Daabu more than three months before its bonfire ceremony. But the time and other resources those three months of work required were investments in more than a single bonfire: from the outset, the ceremonies were only intended to be a beginning.

Organizing for ownership, trustworthiness, and sustainability

Fambul Tok organized its work at the district level (comparable to the state level in the US), and from there it built ever more localized levels of organizing, from the district to the chiefdom (like a county) to the section (a collection of villages) to the village. All of these became long-term, embedded local committee structures, and all of them were made up of volunteers. These structures would later become a critical force in responding to the Ebola crisis of 2014–2016 and in grounding locally led recovery and development thereafter.

When Fambul Tok began working in a new district, it hired three to four people from that district to oversee the efforts there, leading with and from their local context, culture, and languages. They joined a small national staff based in Freetown that worked across all the districts. The real heartbeat of the work, however, was the volunteer structure established in each district, which guaranteed local ownership and long-term sustainability of the work. These volunteer structures were anchored by the District Executive, a committee of equal numbers of men and women that held ultimate responsibility for coordinating and communicating about the *fambul tok* reconciliation process throughout the district. Co-led by a chairman and a chairlady, the District Executive worked with the Fambul Tok national and district staff to identify and prioritize the communities they should approach.

If those communities wanted to join the process, the staff and District Executive helped them set up Reconciliation Committees and Outreach Committees, sectional-level structures responsible for organizing the bonfire and its follow-up activities. The Outreach Committees were made up mostly of youth, who were charged with getting the word out about the ceremony and the larger process that Fambul Tok was facilitating. The Reconciliation Committees were composed of trusted and respected individuals, seen as the informal community "elders" (though there were youth representatives too), who would tend the process in their communities in an ongoing way. Though each Reconciliation Committee was intended to include men and women, Muslims and Christians, elders and youth, victims and perpetrators, the key criterion was that its members were seen by the community as people who worked on behalf of the greater whole, and whom the community held in special trust and respect. Identifying and organizing these folks—Fambul Tok's foundational facilitative work—was like adding yeast to flour and water: it activated a positive growth capacity that touched the whole.

All of the committees received special training in reconciliation and in the Fambul Tok values and process. With support from the Fambul Tok staff, they then led the planning and implementation of the bonfires and the cleansing ceremonies.

An important criterion for membership in these committees was being nonpolitical and nonpartisan. Sierra Leone is intensely politicized, and it is easy for politicians to co-opt almost anything for their own purposes. From the beginning, Fambul Tok was resolute in its commitment to create a different kind of public space. Being nonpolitical and nonpartisan was the only way to open a trusted space, and without that trust, the work simply couldn't go forward. The staff were vigilant in reinforcing this value, in committee selection, and in their own behavior. For example, staff members couldn't wear green or red—the colors associated with the main political parties—when visiting a community, lest they be perceived as representing a party.

The composition of the committees took on heightened importance because they were intended to remain in place after the ceremonies. From the start, Fambul Tok made it clear that a ceremony would signal not the end of reconciliation but the beginning of an ongoing communal process. The Reconciliation Committees helped plan and implement follow-up activities to support and sustain reconciliation and the networks of connection that had been (re)established during the bonfires. Some of these activities, such as soccer matches and "discos," were one-time events, offering people a space to play and relax side by side. Other activities and programs were designed to be integrated into the communities in an ongoing way, such as community farms—common in the past but dormant since the war. Once reestablished, they became spaces where victims and perpetrators could work side by side, in normal interaction, and where communities could continue to develop and exercise their collective decision-making, from choosing crops to selecting land to apportioning the harvest and its proceeds. Communities also designated "peace trees," which offered shelter when villagers gathered to address conflicts that might arise as reconciliation unfolded. The ubiquitous mango trees not only provided much-needed shade from the sweltering sun but also delimited a symbolic, ongoing, living space for the collective—a space where the roots, branches, earth, and people form a symbiotic whole.

Centering women, mothering peace

Sections, the collections of villages where Fambul Tok centered its organizing, also established Peace Mothers groups, a space for women to come together in informal conversation and support. These groups naturally oriented themselves outward, taking on projects to better their communities as a whole. They became engines of community development, simultaneously driving and being fueled by the places they embraced in their projects. Later, they became integral to responding meaningfully to the Ebola outbreak. And yet, even with an express commitment to equal representation, the original *fambul tok* design hadn't included Peace Mothers groups— the idea came from community women themselves.

From the beginning, every Fambul Tok activity was done with attention to gender equality. The volunteer structures always had equal numbers of men and women, and in stakeholder and planning meetings, Fambul Tok staff made explicit and repeated efforts to invite women to speak, to model and reinforce what it took to have women's voices be fully part of the public space. But in the early days of the program, there was a rumble from more and more women that even having equal representation in these commit-tees was not enough. Because of the unique way they had suffered during the war, as well as the systemic and ongoing discrimina-tion against women in Sierra Leone, they wanted something more to support their ongoing healing and recovery. So Fambul Tok did what it always did—it gathered those impacted from across its active program areas to ask, listen, and learn what more they wanted and needed.

Fambul Tok hosted a cross-section of women in Kailahun Town, and for many of them, it was the first time they had traveled outside their villages. As always, their jubilation led the way. The women began circling each other with song and dance as soon as they arrived—a swirling ocean of joyous color. Eventually, without any visible coordination, the singing quieted, and they moved into the circle of seats to share more stories—often for the first time—of what had happened to them in the war. "I don't think I can tell my story in words," one young woman said quietly. "So I'm going to sing it." She sang into the circle about how she was violated during the war, and the circle held her—literally and figuratively.

The weight of any one of their stories alone was heavy, and the collective weight was almost unbearable. What kind of sup-port might help meet the needs of these women? With Fambul Tok's light facilitative touch, the conversation shifted from shar-ing stories to thinking together about that question. The women said they simply wanted an ongoing space to gather, as women. Not lots of special programming. Not formalized structures and official-sounding names—politicized spaces they had seen co-opted in the past. They wanted to channel their pain by working together, as women, for the benefit of their communities. And they decided they wanted to be called Peace Mothers.

From that moment, the Peace Mothers became embedded in the *fambul tok* reconciliation process, one of the structures that Fambul Tok would help each community create during the ceremony planning process. With little external support other than help in launching their initial meetings and activities, the Peace Mothers became the vital engine of community rebirth, reenergizing a new-old community ethic of togetherness, where everyone worked together on behalf of the whole. They infused a spirit into their communities—a generosity, an outward orientation, and a fierce refusal to let the past define or limit them or their communities. "They don't think about themselves and their children or their husbands only," John observed. "They think about the community. They want schools—for the community. They think about a hospital—for the community. They think about creating an income-generating scheme—to support the community. Unlike men. Men, we mostly think about . . . ourselves. It's just my wife, my kids. But the women are helping to shift that discourse into a community thing."

The Peace Mothers' story both embodies and suggests new definitions of power. Author and educator Susie Herrick observes that this kind of feminine, female-led power is "not a power we're used to; it is not a power that seeks to dominate or . . . to rule the world, or . . . to be number one despite everything. [It's] a totally different power. It's a power of love. A power of wanting the whole to thrive. To have a place where people can bring out who they are and be in a chorus with everyone else."[1] The Peace Mothers' work and their voices, vision, and insistence gave space, outside the private realm, to the networks of care and affection that ground the basic work of the family. They (re)created a space in the public arena to operate on behalf of the community. The result has been an unleashing of new energies and impact and a vital and vibrant example of feminine, female-led power in action.

Becoming the container

All of these elements—Reconciliation Committees, community farms, soccer matches, peace trees, Peace Mothers, and more—are like microcommunities that support and sustain war-impacted individuals. Taken together, these living structures represent a strong, revitalized, *whole* community—whether fully realized or still in process—that is itself a circle of support for the individuals within it. It was this newly (re)claimed whole that became the fireproof container strong enough to host and hold the storytelling, forgiveness, and ongoing work of moving forward together.

And it is, indeed, an *ongoing process*.

In Daabu, where the ruins of the community's *court barray* had dominated landscape and memory, the bonfire opened space that allowed the community to come together afterward and rebuild the *barray*. Without waiting for outside help, community members started with what they had in abundance: dirt and labor. They

---

1   Chantal Pierrat, "Your Story Is Your Power with Elle Luna and Susie Herrick," April 3, 2018, in *The Emerging Women Podcast*, produced by Emerging Women, podcast, 1:06:01, https://emergingwomen.com/podcast/elle-luna-susie-herrick/.

began to make mud bricks, and soon, rows upon rows of bricks were drying in the sun. Villagers cleared land and began a community farm to generate funds for the roof, turning overgrown bushlands into fertile fields in the name of the community. Victims and perpetrators, ex-rebels and civilians, worked side by side to plant, tend, harvest, and market their crops. With the proceeds from the harvest, they bought zinc sheets for the roof, and together they framed and rebuilt their community center. Today, the *barray* stands as a vibrant gathering center for the village, a visible reminder of the idea it embodies—the vitality of whole community. And the process of building it embodied the community's wholeness as much as the physical building itself does now.

On the literal, physical level, Daabu didn't have anything more after the bonfire than before. But what the community did regain was a sense of its wholeness, of its collective identity beyond what the war had done to it. The bonfire—and, crucially, the process of preparing for it—had helped the village reclaim its identity as a living entity serving and supporting the greater good by supporting all its residents, even through the horrors they had experienced. The living body of the community did what only it could do: it restored dignity to both the victims and the perpetrators of the violence. The public confessions restored victims' dignity, and the public acceptance restored the same for those perpetrators who confessed. They could once again become "good somebodies," as one ex-combatant put it, in the eyes of their community.

This was not merely a restoration. This post-bonfire Daabu was not the same community that had existed before the war; it couldn't be. But a new community was (re)born, with new kinds of connectedness. Old norms were challenged, including those around the accountability of chiefs or the leadership of women. The larger purpose of community healing brought everyone together, valued everyone equally, and laid equal responsibility on each for the progress they wanted to make collectively. That shifted the ground, and people felt the presence of a greater whole that invited them *all* forward. This reborn (sense of) community became like an underground wellspring, inspiring and nourishing new activity and engagement for the betterment of all, like the community farm and the rebuilding of the *barray*. And through nearly 250 bonfire ceremonies, the pattern repeated in village after village across the country.

It can be easy for any of us to feel overwhelmed by the brokenness of the communities we are working with, as it was for me when I first entered Daabu. But my experience with Fambul Tok has shown me that once we understand what community wholeness is, its power becomes available to draw from and use, even after terrible tragedy. The wholeness of the community is not simply a goal to attain at some future point. It *also exists in the present as a resource*, even in the midst of visible brokenness and devastation. If we ask and imagine what an already whole and healthy community would do—how it would respond to present challenges—then we can work in a way that embodies those qualities *already*, and we can create the structures that will sustain the community in the long term. Listening and acting from the perspective of community wholeness enables us to tap into a deeper wisdom. This idea, too, would be confirmed in village after village, year after year—in moments when great crises, like Ebola, birthed great possibilities.

Chapter 6

SAYING, AND HEARING, HARD THINGS

Foendor is a tiny farming community consisting of only a handful of homes in Kono District, the heart of Sierra Leone's diamond mining industry, north of Kailahun and on the country's eastern edge. Before the war, Foendor was a quiet community, surrounded by rich farmlands that were the focus of daily life for its residents. But the war inflicted a particular brutality on the people of Foendor. Even in a district notorious for the bloody struggle over its diamonds, a struggle that fueled the civil war and the regional power play surrounding it, the devastation in Foendor stands out as horrific. On the lands where he grew up, Tamba Joe killed and beheaded 17 members of his extended family, a crime that touched all the residents of Foendor, where "neighbor" and "family" are essentially the same thing. Those who survived couldn't face returning to their village, and Foendor's small circle of mud-brick, thatched-roof homes lay deserted and crumbling, several of the nearby fields abandoned.

Even a decade after the massacre, the pain of its memory nearly overwhelmed the *fambul tok* consultation process that began there in January of 2009. As community members talked together about whether and how to reopen these wounds, they were in fact peeling back the bandages already. The Fambul Tok staff and local leaders listened carefully for whether community members wanted to proceed with the process and, if so, in what manner. As painful as those conversations were, they also began to strengthen the community container, preparing it to hold brutal truths of the war with honesty, courage, compassion, and faith. After several days of conversation, the people of Foendor committed to a *fambul tok* bonfire and reconciliation process. They didn't know what its outcome would be, but they shared a conviction that it carried important potential for their individual and communal healing.

The consultation process and the community organizing that followed opened a clear and genuine desire for Tamba Joe to return. He hadn't been seen or heard from since the war, but the community wanted him to speak to them directly. Together with Fambul Tok staff, people from Foendor spent months traveling the country in search of Tamba Joe, putting the word out about the bonfire and inviting him to come forward, tell his story, and apologize, with the understanding that there was the possibility of being forgiven and welcomed back into his community. Their efforts, and the spirit in which they were made, expressed an extraordinary, almost unimaginable, generosity and hope.

Though the bonfire began without Tamba Joe, there was hope

even as the ceremony went on that he might appear. Sahr Foendor was the first to testify, sharing that his mother and infant daughter were among those whom Tamba Joe had killed. He spoke slowly, pausing several times as he recounted the events of the day. When he finished, the moderator called out for Tamba Joe to come forward. The crowd waited through a dramatic silence, but Tamba Joe did not appear.

Instead, his three sisters, who still lived in the community, came forward on his behalf. They encircled Sahr Foendor and apologized for what their brother had done, kneeling and begging for forgiveness. Sahr Foendor softly touched the tops of their bowed heads and accepted their apology. The four quietly locked arms and walked slowly out of the center of the circle, each leaning into and supporting the other.

Their healing journey, and Foendor's as a whole, continued well after the ceremony. Sahr Foendor and the Joe sisters, with the support of their community, decided they wanted to build a memorial in the place where the killings had taken place, and they worked together to plan and construct it. As they did, the formerly abandoned town and farmlands were slowly reclaimed, homes repaired and reinhabited. Foendor became an active farming village once again.

The full story of Foendor's experience is chronicled in our 2011 feature film, *Fambul Tok*. Sara and the rest of the film crew documented the unfolding story patiently, over many months and several trips to Sierra Leone, and the heartrending realities of every part of the process pulse through the film. After the bonfire, Sara interviewed Naomi Joe, one of Tamba Joe's sisters. She asked Naomi if she had a message for her brother—if he was ever found. Speaking softly in her native Kono, her answer came out like a poem of love and heartbreak.

I have a message.

What I have to tell him—don't be afraid.

Anything can happen for us. And everything has an end.

There is time for crying.

There is time for death.

There is time for happiness.

I believe that with our apology at the bonfire for the role that you played, I feel that we have been forgiven.

So wherever you are, you should not be afraid to come home. But if you are not ready to come, let there at least be some communication between us.

Now we have taken the responsibility to work together as a family.

We have lost enough of our relatives in the war.

Our mother is now dead.

Our father is dead.

Our cousins died.

Even our own children died in this war. A lot of them.

*Please come home so that we can do some cleansing and
sacrifices to all who died.*

That is all I have to say.[2]

As far as we know, Naomi Joe's message never reached her
brother, who still has not been found. In an unlikely series of events,
however, it did make its way to another son of Kono, Captain
Mohamed Savage.

Mohamed Savage, once known as "Mr. Die," was one of the
most notorious fighters in the war, and human rights groups argued
for his inclusion in the list of top commanders to be prosecuted by
the Special Court. A large pond in Tombodu, the town next to
Foendor, was known as "Savage Pit," and it was where Captain
Savage dumped the bodies of those he had killed. It was where
Sahr Foendor's wife had been forced to carry and leave a bag of all
the decapitated heads from the Foendor massacre, including the
head of her own child.

In 2009, Mohamed Savage was released after serving nine years
in a government prison, not connected to the Special Court process, for other crimes he had committed late in the war. Learning
of his release, Sara wanted to interview him about Tamba Joe and
the events in Foendor. John arranged the meeting a few days before
the end of the film crew's final trip to Sierra Leone. But Savage
flatly denied knowing Tamba Joe or anything about the massacre
at Foendor. He even denied his own identity, insisting he wasn't

---

2 *Fambul Tok*, directed by Sara Terry (2011; Portland, ME: Catalyst for Peace),
documentary.

that Mohamed Savage. He'd never even been to Kono, he said, or anywhere near the places those atrocities had happened. Needless to say, the interview ended quickly.

A few hours later, however, Savage requested another meeting the following day. Again, he began with denials. John and Sara explained that if he *were* that Savage, even he could be welcomed back to Kono if he wanted to acknowledge, and apologize for, what he had done. John told him how he had an opportunity to choose a different path now, and how he could play a role in helping bring peace to Sierra Leone by leading the way for high-level command-ers to apologize and reconcile.

Still, he denied everything.

Then Sara showed him Naomi Joe's message to her brother. Headphones on, he watched the video on Sara's laptop. His eyes twitched, and his breath shortened. His demeanor com-pletely changed. Yet still, when he took off the headphones, he denied everything.

Sara and the crew packed up, ready to fly out the following evening. That night, Savage called John three times. He wanted to talk again, one more time.

So the next morning, with bags packed and loaded into the car, the film crew and John met Savage again. This time, he began by acknowledging who he was and what he had done. He said he wanted to go back to Tombodu and apologize for what he had done during the war. He said that he felt Naomi Joe's message had been aimed directly at him, and it had reached him right in the heart. "I must reconcile with my people," he said. "I must."

Mohamed Savage remained committed to going back and owning up to what he had done in the war, and to beginning a reconciliation process with his community. Fambul Tok committed to supporting that process, knowing it would be different from any of the previous bonfires. And then Fambul Tok discovered that even though the Special Court was winding down, it could still issue indictments. It was possible that Savage's testimony at a *fambul tok* bonfire could be used to indict him. Though Savage was willing to take that risk, John was not, knowing it could undermine Fambul Tok's credibility and its ability to ensure the safety of the *fambul tok* bonfire spaces going forward.

The perpetrator was ready to testify, to accept whatever consequences his community might offer, and to begin what would surely be a long process of reconciliation and reengagement. And the official international justice mechanisms were an obstacle to that process—a painful irony, and one that we assumed was the end of the story.

Eighteen months later, however, Savage could wait no longer. He still wanted Fambul Tok's help, but he said he would go forward no matter what. Despite the risks, Fambul Tok decided to facilitate the process. Community consultation began around Tombodu to find out if the village would be willing to host such a process and, if so, to prepare the ground. At first, Paramount Chief Aiah Melvin Ngekia did not even want to see Savage. The paramount chief, as well as the town and section chiefs, debated the question vigorously. They were uncertain if Savage should return or if they wanted to open up a public testimony process at all, and they sought broad input on the question. But the people in their chiefdom made it clear that they wanted Savage to return and testify. Many weren't certain they would be able to forgive him, but they wanted *him* to hear *them* tell about the pain he had caused, and they wanted to hear his reply. Eventually, even Chief Ngekia came around to supporting the process.

And so, on November 12, 2010, the community of Tombodu hosted hundreds of people from across the chiefdom for a bonfire specifically for Mohamed Savage and presided over by Chief Ngekia. As the night sky darkened and the flames danced, person after person testified about what he had done to them or their family members; Savage sat and listened, with obvious pain in his face. When it was his turn to speak, he used a megaphone so that everyone could hear him. Still, the crowd closed in, hardly believing it could actually be Mohamed Savage.

Commander Savage got down on bended knee and asked the paramount chief and the crowd for their forgiveness. He acknowledged, and took responsibility for, what he had done during the war, including everything that others had done while under his command. He described the good intentions he had had to serve his country when he joined the military and how the war had corrupted those intentions. If he had known what would happen, he said, he never would have joined the military. He said he understood that not everyone he harmed could testify that night, nor could he respond that night to each individual accusation. But he offered to meet with anyone who wanted to speak with him in the coming weeks and months. He said he knew this wouldn't be a quick process, and he expressed his commitment to engage for as long as it took. Still on his knees, he again begged for forgiveness, and he pleaded for everyone to move forward together so that the community could hold the peace "with two hands"—by those who had harmed and those who had been harmed.

Paramount Chief Ngekia stood and took the megaphone. On

behalf of the entire chiefdom, he accepted Savage's apology and offered forgiveness.

People pressed forward to catch a glimpse of Savage's face, and the crowd murmured with excitement, ultimately forcing the organizers to cut the evening short to ensure everyone's safety. But the purpose had been accomplished. Savage was welcomed back to Tombodu. The communal cleansing ceremony at Savage Pit the day after the bonfire certainly didn't erase the memories or impact of its ghastly legacy. But it signaled the beginning of the community's reclamation of that space, and the opening chapter of a new story the people of Tombodu might write together. Savage found an apartment, played and coached soccer, and began life anew in many ways, as did Tombodu.

Later, Savage joined the Fambul Tok staff, eager for any way he could make a contribution to supporting the organization's work. He did significant work with other ex-combatants, which I will describe later in the book. But much of his time with Fambul Tok was about simply showing up to support whatever needed to be done in the office. His willingness to do outwardly menial work, in relative anonymity, was seen not as a sign of weakness but rather as the living out of a different kind of strength.

All of this was only made possible because of Fambul Tok's fundamental commitment to repairing community, and to trusting a renewed community to hold and alchemize even the fiercest truths of the war. Community is the place where people are connected not by position or role but simply by their fundamental humanness, and it is our very humanness that contains the seeds for transformation and healing. In fact, the reclamation of our humanity after experiencing, or even causing, great harm *is* the transformation.

Foendor and Tombodu showed how strong and powerful the yearning is to speak and to hear truth, even really hard truths, and that truth-speak—trusting others with our hard truths, and being trusted with theirs in turn—is experienced as a restoration of dignity, of humanity.

The commitment to being human, even after horror; the commitment to invite and allow someone else to be human, even after unspeakable tragedy—these are among the most powerful forces on the planet. We need each other in order to invite and invoke that power. And we need ways of being together that can help us do it.

Part II

A PEACE-BUILDER'S JOURNEY

I was supposed to be in Bosnia. Or Belfast. Or rural Kenya or Nigeria, studying how people use religion as a resource for peace, even in the midst of violence. I was supposed to be working at the pioneering frontiers of peacebuilding, bridging the chasm between the Muslim and Christian worlds, or the centuries-long divide between Catholics and Protestants in Northern Ireland. Instead, I was in Alton, Illinois, a sleepy town in the middle of heartland America. And I was watching my small congregation descend into bitter, destructive conflict over the church's position on homosexuality.

It was 1999, still the early years after the Cold War. I was writing my dissertation about religion and peacebuilding, exploring the ways faith communities were uniquely poised to bring ordinary people into the work of peace. I also thought religion's capacity to bring moral authority and to invite and infuse moral courage into elite-level politics was little understood, much less intentionally cultivated. Policy communities were anchored in a secular Western liberal paradigm that simply didn't know what to do with religion and therefore pretty much chose to ignore it.

I, on the other hand, wanted to dive in. But I was stuck. I couldn't quite summon the courage to take my elementary-aged kids abroad for a year of field research, and I couldn't imagine being apart from them for that long. I felt pulled in opposite directions—my core commitment to home and family and mothering tugging against a strong call to international peacebuilding, which I knew required on-the-ground experience. And the pieces just weren't coming together in ways I could see or feel comfortable about. I felt torn. And confused. Which brought out my self-doubt.

As I always did in times of great challenge, I turned to prayer for direction. My regular practice was to bring my internal questions to my daily study of the Bible and *Science and Health with Key to the Scriptures*, the companion textbook of Christian Science, praying with the guidance they offered. I tried to listen from a deeper place for trustworthy purpose—both my own and in the most universal sense. An upcoming trip to a professional peacebuilding conference gave me time away from busy work and family life, and I used it to focus my prayer more intentionally.

On the last day of the conference, with my books and my journal beside me on the bed and still no clear sense of direction, the only prayer I could muster was just a question: What do I need to understand? In that moment of receptivity, this answer came with ringing clarity: it is easier to *plan* for peace for the whole world, *tomorrow*, than to take the opportunities we have to *make* peace, *today*.

Sigh.

I was being asked to let go of the glamour of the global and instead listen for and lean into opportunities to make peace in my everyday life. I was also reminded that I wanted to *be* a peacebuilder, not just think and write about peace. *Being* a peacebuilder requires cultivating the qualities it takes to help transform violence. That's an inside job, one that's as much about who we are as it is about what talents, skills, or expertise we have. And it's a job that can be done anywhere we are, if we allow it. When I got the chance to put that to the test in my small-town church (stay tuned), the lessons became foundational.

Being and *doing* have been in generative tension for me throughout my journey as a peacebuilder. At times they feel oppositional, but I focus on using that tension to weave them together, like strands in a braid, into a whole that is stronger and more beautiful. I weave the intellectual and the spiritual, the public and the private, the individual and the communal. I begin by digging beneath the opposition I can see or feel on the surface, and then I look for complementarity. Then, I weave. I don't always succeed at first. Sometimes I make a mess of knots, and then I have to untangle and reweave.

But that is the journey.

Chapter 7

HEAD "VERSUS" HEART

I love learning. That, probably more than anything else, is the unifying thread running through my life. My sister, Melissa, was my first teacher, and so my hero. Two years older, she would come home from school every day and teach me what she had learned. Wide-eyed and eager, I soaked it all up, my short little legs swinging back and forth a good foot above the red-and-blue shag carpet under the family-room game table. I still remember the thrill of feeling the oversize red pencil, fat between my fingers, and watching it make marks on the wide-ruled paper. I grew up thinking school must be the most important thing in the world, because once Melissa started going, she assumed the place of honor at the dinner table. Every night, Mom and Dad prodded her to share what she was learning. They regularly added new information to her lessons, or quizzed her on math, games I was eager to join as well. By the time I started school, the quizzes at dinner fed me as much as the food. I remember the night my parents explained negative numbers, which, as far as I was concerned, were as close to real-world magic as you could get. Not long after, my teacher miswrote a math problem on the board as "4 – 9" instead of "4 + 9," and I took special delight in pointing out that the answer was –5, but since we hadn't studied negative numbers yet, I didn't think she meant to put that on the board. I had gone to kindergarten already knowing how to read (and eager to tell my teacher and anyone else who would listen), and I skipped second grade entirely, thanks to my sister and to our dinner-table learning lab.

My parents prized knowledge right up there with virtue as among the most important things to cultivate in this world. For them, the value of learning was always linked with a clear sense of its ultimate purpose—to help us make a better contribution to the world. My parents emphasized that this was the underlying goal of education and ultimately the reason we were all on this planet. It was just as clear to me, though, that learning itself brought out my parents' pride and approval, and sometimes more material rewards. When I was ten or eleven, my dad made me a deal: I could earn a quarter for every new vocabulary word I learned if I could say the definition and then use the word in a sentence. I got fifty cents if it was a word in *Science and Health*. I was no dummy. I went straight to the concordance to *Science and Health* and looked through it methodically for words I didn't know. My dad offered me the top prize of a dollar for words he didn't already know. In a testament to his own love of learning, I only stumped him once (and I can understand why *agamogenesis* wouldn't have been in his regular vocabulary). It's no wonder that learning brought out all my competitive juices, or that it wasn't always easy for me to tell the difference between what others thought was important (or at least what I *thought* they thought) and what *I* thought was important.

My curiosity was a thirst that could never be quenched. I had learned from my earliest days how to find knowledge outside of myself, but my first summer at camp, when I was nine, I also experienced a different kind of learning—and with it a different dimension of curiosity. Camp Kohahna is a camp for Christian Scientists on the shores of the magical Leelanau Peninsula on Lake Michigan, where white-sand beaches and wide horizons of blue-green water make it feel like being at the ocean. The summer ends with a banquet, where one older and one younger camper are selected by the camp staff to give short inspirational talks on a spiritual idea important to them. I was simultaneously proud and petrified to be asked to give the younger camper's talk, and I told my counselor I had no idea what I should say. She looked at me with calm confidence and said, "You'll know! Just listen for what comes to you." Her matter-of-factness settled my fears and opened my thought to the possibility of the truth of what she said.

So I took my journal into the woods, where I found a clearing among the white pines and settled onto a soft cushion of pine needles. I lay back, looking up at the sky through the gaps in the treetops. The sun shone down on me, and I rested a moment in its warmth. Then it hit me. Those trees didn't have to worry about how or where to grow. The sun warmed them, just like it was warming me, and they effortlessly grew toward its light. I realized it was the same for me, for all of us; our spiritual progress could be just as effortless. I felt a sense of divine light, of goodness, of Love, calling us all to grow in its direction, and it felt natural for us to do just that. I shared that insight at the banquet.

Though I received nice feedback about my speech, I had no illusions of it changing anyone's life. But the experience of doing it changed *my* life. The invitation and support from the camp leaders showed me that, even as a nine-year-old girl, I could know and share spiritual wisdom in my community. It was the first time I experienced a communal learning space that invited me and others to discover and share our inner wisdom, and I internalized a sense that the very universe itself was issuing me the same invitation. I left camp knowing that I could lean into the warmth of that invitation whenever and wherever I heard it, and that it would cultivate deep learning and new growth.

That inner listening was sometimes hard for me to prioritize in a formal school setting, where the focus on individual achievement, and the pull of extrinsic motivations (Gold stars! Good grades! Awards! Opportunities!), nurtured my drive to learn "the most" and be "the best." I found success by cultivating and demonstrating my expertise, which suited my competitive instincts well. While this was helpful in some ways, it also stifled my own thinking and creativity. One time in seventh-grade English, when I was assigned to craft a one-page description of something from my daily life, I froze and couldn't write *anything*. By Saturday morning, I had a growing pile of crumpled paper from ill-fated attempts, and I went to my mom in tears for help. Looking up from the sitting-room couch in her kaftan robe, cradling her favorite Staffordshire "Calico Blue" mug, she noticed the antique gold-leafed mirror on the wall. "Why don't you write about that?" she asked. She helped me come up with verbal flourishes as gilded as the mirror. Since she had been an English major in college, I convinced myself that this idea must be good and that using fancy words about a fancy mirror would surely "win first prize" (which, of course, only existed in my imagination). When it came time to read my paper aloud in class, I felt like somebody else's words were coming out of my mouth. The red heat of embarrassment rose from my neck to the top of my head, and I wanted to hide in the back of the room. I felt so jealous of Tam Eady's simple, elegant prose about a funny but bittersweet family moment, and although I smugly dismissed Rick Dreyer's work as slipshod, at least he was writing about his passion, even if it was something as unimportant as golf. I realized I didn't know how to begin to write about what I enjoyed or appreciated. I wasn't sure I even knew what that was.

The inner call I heard even at a young age to work internationally seemed to make centering my own wisdom even harder, in part because my view of international affairs as a career was so limited. In high school, I dreamed of being secretary of state or vice president of an international bank. (One had visited my family growing up, and he'd seemed exceedingly glamorous.) At Williams College, where I was majoring in political science, I decided to minor in Russian studies, not so much because I liked Russian or wanted to learn about the country or the culture, but because, at the height of the Cold War, I thought that knowing Russian would give me access to the most important issues of the day. A ticket to the highest echelons of foreign policy work. An express train to the top of the political power pyramid.

And yet my most pivotal college learning experience was nowhere on that pyramid. A class on nonviolence in theory and practice offered me new insights into power through its content and pedagogy. In the opening pages of *The Politics of Nonviolent Action*, the seminal work in the field and primary textbook of our class, Gene Sharp describes how nonviolent theory flips conventional thinking about power. "The exercise of power depends on the consent of the ruled who, by withdrawing that consent, can control and even destroy the power of their opponent," Sharp wrote.[3] The power is actually in our consent—which only we control. For the first time, I was reading political theory that seemed totally in line with one of my core convictions, rooted in my faith: that nothing outside us inherently has power over us, and that we have not only the right but also the obligation to challenge the legitimacy of anything that tries to say otherwise. By reconceptualizing power, Sharp defined the public arena in a way that recognized ordinary people as primary actors. I saw how that meant there was a space for *me*, as a person, and specifically a space for my thinking and consciousness, my inner self.

The structure and process of the class also taught me about power in an embodied way. The course was organized and run by students. We took turns leading class discussions, and I relished the opportunity to conceptualize and facilitate, although it also felt foreign and a bit scary. When I wasn't facilitating, I remember feeling that my contributions were important and needed. I experienced the very format of the class as an invitation to contribute and as an affirmation of the importance of my own thinking and experience. Although there were none of the traditional extrinsic rewards—no letter grades, for example—I never worked harder or felt like I learned more. The lesson wasn't lost on me: learning spaces are political spaces. How we structure them impacts who we can be and how and what we can learn.

---

3   Gene Sharp, *The Politics of Nonviolent Action, Part One: Power and Struggle* (Boston: Porter Sargent Publishers, 1973), 4.

My father understood very little of this, however. How could a class be valuable if it wasn't taught by an esteemed professor? What exactly was he paying all this money for, anyway, if we were left to teach ourselves? He called it my "non-sense" class instead of my nonviolence class. And he was mortified when I helped initiate an advanced-level class on strategic nonviolence the following year.

The (dinner) tables turned. At our family meals, my sister and I took on the role of teaching our parents, and my dad in particular. I would have been happy to ignore my dad's bluster and simply go on about my business, and my education, in spite of it. Melissa was always braver about initiating direct confrontation, however, and I was happy to move in her wake, once again learning from her experience and, in the process, becoming a better advocate for my ideas. These moments followed something of a script: My father sat at the head of our large antique mahogany dining table, and when a controversial topic came up, he would push his chair away, lean back with his head slightly cocked and his legs stretched out in front of him, and relax his arms on the padded dining chair like it was his throne. That was Melissa's cue to lob a fact she knew would challenge him—about discrimination against women, or the militarization of society, or environmental degradation, or whatever the night's topic was. Dad would sit up a little straighter and toss out a dismissive quip or perhaps a categorical denial. I would come in with a question inviting thoughtful reflection on his underlying values and vision for the world. And back and forth we went, until he was leaning in right along with us, elbows on the table or arms gesticulating while making a point. My mom occasionally joined the debate, as likely on our side as on Dad's. But just as often, she watched, her closed-mouthed smile and the twinkle in her eye signaling how much she relished seeing her daughters being and becoming our lively, engaged, and engaging selves. When Dad interrupted or patronized us, we'd call him out. We insisted on getting verbal confirmation that he had actually understood what we said before letting him respond with a counterargument, and we did the same for him.

My dad might not have had an intellectual framework for validating our perspectives or experience, but I knew his love for us, his love for humanity, and his desire to serve were all deep and true. I wanted to converse with his heart, not just his head, and to grow the conversation from there. My favorite conversations were those in which we stood side by side facing a common challenge, each bringing our own perspective but knowing clearly that we were working together on the same issue. We all learned, practiced, and advocated for a vigorous engagement around difference that was, bottom line, respectful of all of us as people and as thinkers. A dinner-table learning lab indeed.

Chapter 8

BODIES POLITIC

After college, I planned to head to Washington, DC, and begin my world-changing work, whatever that might be. But I fell in love and got married the summer I graduated. I moved not to Washington but to southern Illinois, where my new husband was coaching soccer and baseball at Principia College, a small campus just across the Mississippi from St. Louis. Part of me was OK with moving there. And part of me felt that by prioritizing family, I was being banished to the Midwest and consigned to a life of no consequence. And soft, white bread.

It wasn't until I had been married a few years that I warmed to the idea of having children. Prior to that, I was sure I didn't want them—if I'm honest, I didn't even like children very much—but watching friends have babies opened me up to the possibility. By the time I was 24, I was ready. The irony is not lost on me: it took living a thousand miles from the centers of power to make space for the part of me committed to the nurturing and care of others to come to the fore. I had followed my heart to the heartland, but my head had made lots of noise. Thankfully, despite my head's delusions of grandeur, the whole of my body called the shots. I could almost hear my body saying, "Listen, sweetheart. You don't understand this yet, but your heart does. I'm going to begin the conversation with your heart, and then we'll grow it from there. Trust me on this—you're still missing some important ideas, and you don't even know it yet. Someday you'll get it too, and our whole will be in sync."

I still remained committed to my international calling, but now, pregnant with my first child, I was as thrilled to start a family as I was to be heading back to Boston for graduate school.

By the time I began my coursework at the Fletcher School of Law and Diplomacy at Tufts University, my core academic interests included gender and feminist theory. I thought it was a huge problem that women's experiences and agency were missing from conceptualizations of international relations, and I appreciated that feminist scholarship made those things visible. I felt called by the very notion of a field of study that emerged from what had been traditionally excluded. What did it take to uncover ideas and experiences ignored or devalued by a dominant system, and then to use them as the starting point for inquiry, reflection, and theory-building? I wanted to learn from those who claimed space that wasn't given to them, those who were told in all sorts of direct and indirect ways, "You don't matter. You don't count. You don't *exist*."

My years at Fletcher overlapped with the fall of the Soviet Union, which was unthinkable when I enrolled and imminent by the time I graduated. The Cold War was ending and, with it, many of our assumptions about international security and the role of nation-states. Increasingly, wars were civil wars or insurgencies, fought by nontraditional and often non-state fighters, but our international system still viewed the state as the primary actor, which made it difficult to respond to the changing circumstances. Meanwhile, ordinary people were increasingly impacted by war and violent conflict—and they were mostly ignored in the work of building peace. And yet, it was *people* power that had brought down communism in Eastern Europe.

Leaky breasts

As global changes reordered the world, changes in my family, and in my very body, reordered my life. I was pregnant with my first child during my first semester of graduate school. As the Iron Curtain crumbled, my belly grew. Besides the humor of having to sit sideways in order to fit into the classroom desks, my pregnancy was a visceral reminder to me of what I knew at some level was *really* most important—a human life in its most singular, intimate, and personal form. I was beginning to see and feel the ways motherhood was not just expanding my body but opening up new space in my thought, inviting me into new understandings of the world around me.

I started spring semester two weeks after my son Caleb was born. One day in Contemporary European Security, just as we were discussing emerging channels for security cooperation, I felt my breasts start to leak. Not unusual for a new mother, of course, but in the classroom, it felt jarring and slightly absurd, which heightened my awareness of it and my desire to disappear into invisibility at the time. I soon forgot about it, but today it is one of those insistent memories poking at my consciousness, inviting a new seeing. My leaky breasts weren't just a personal and individual thing. Rather, my body was showing me something that neither my head nor the course syllabus had caught up to yet—that feeding babies is very much a part of contemporary European security. Of security *anywhere*. In that Fletcher classroom, my body was reminding me that there is power and importance in small actions of care and nurturing. That nourishment could be perfectly formulated from within and didn't need to be brought in from the outside. That I had what I needed. And that these things are just as important as cease-fire agreements and interoperability strategies. A quote from Jean Bethke Elshtain's *Women and War* went up on my bulletin board, where it stayed for many years: "I hoped inchoately that I might one day put together mothering and political thinking rather than have to put aside the one in order to engage in the other."[4]

The twin pulls of career and family—a desire to engage in globally important work and also to tend and nurture a family— continued, and by the time I received my master's degree, I was pregnant with my second son. This time, I couldn't wait to get back to the Midwest. I didn't want to raise my children in a place that I felt would force them to grow up too fast, and one so utterly lacking in open space and friendly neighbors to boot.

So we moved back to Illinois, where, after a few years of raising babies and finishing my PhD coursework, I became the first female political science professor at Principia College, and its first political science professor to teach courses in the women's studies program. In

---

4   Jean Bethke Elshtain, *Women and War* (New York: Basic Books, 1987), 32.

all my classes, I looked for ways to peel back the layers on our lives and trace connections to global issues—for example, by using clothing and food-source labels to explore how the intersecting dynamics of global trade, labor laws, regional power politics, and international development were just under the surface in our everyday lives. I always looked for ways to engage and support my students as people, not just as students. I also spoke regularly of my life outside the classroom, and I worked to integrate my mothering self fully into my professional self. I made a point to speak to my classes about the challenges of trying to balance work and family, noting that I was able to be there in part because there was a full-time day care on the college campus. When I was in the middle of giving a lecture on the politics of Southwest Asia and I suddenly remembered that our house was out of toilet paper, I made a mental note to pick some up on the way home—and then told my students about it, as an example of the kind of multitasking that women, especially mothers, do all the time.

This approach to teaching was also part of claiming and constructing, bit by bit, a new kind of public, or political, space. I framed my classroom as a microcosm of the public space, noticing and focusing class discussions on the gender dynamics of class participation, for example. Those conversations, and the incredible resistance they provoked from some (mostly male) students, helped demonstrate the connections between the way the international political system is structured and the assumptions and behavior patterns we play out in our everyday lives. And by refusing to put aside mothering while I was a professor, I was demonstrating that being a political scientist and being a human being weren't mutually exclusive. I hoped that could prepare my students to enter their public lives, however and wherever that happened, as whole, integrated people.

Peacebuilding, meet religion

While teaching an advanced-level course in conflict resolution, I began to discover work I had not been exposed to in graduate school: the pioneering faith-based peacebuilding happening around the world. Although most of it was localized and small-scale, it felt important and full of potential, even while it was underacknowledged and undervalued in my field. I thought the world needed more of it. I began teaching about it in my classes and exploring it with students and peers outside the classroom.

In 1996, I was the faculty advisor for the annual student-run public affairs conference. That year, the students decided to focus on conflict resolution and invited Cynthia Sampson, editor of the pioneering book *Religion: The Missing Dimension of Statecraft*, as a conference speaker. Cynthia was also a Christian Scientist, working at the time at Eastern Mennonite University, where she had helped establish the Center for Justice and Peacebuilding. Cynthia sensed the depth of the students' interest and hosted an informal conversation exploring Christian Science and conflict resolution. It drew an unexpectedly large group. "Why does a Christian Scientist have to have a Mennonite business card?" she asked us with lighthearted humor while pointing out that other denominations had been organizing to bring the resources of their faith to peace work for a long, long time.

That conversation sparked another and then another, held in different Christian Science communities and organizations around the country, as Cynthia and I worked to foster a broader communal dialogue about how to bring our own faith more fully to the work of peace. By late 1999, a little band of spiritual explorers coalesced into a nonprofit organization. Rather than crafting an institutionalized form of "Christian Science peacebuilding," we were drawn to ask if we could offer a space for inviting the highest and best characteristics of *all* faith traditions in their work for peace, and if we could leaven the peacebuilding field as a whole. In choosing the name Peace Discovery Initiatives (PDI), we rejected the dominant language and underlying approach of the field of conflict resolution, which focused on looking for "problems" to "solve." We grounded ourselves in a conviction that peace is a given, not a goal, and we framed peacebuilding as discovering and uncovering the resources for peace we believed were already present, even in places torn by conflict, and even if hidden from view.

We convened a major conference, called Positive Approaches to Peacebuilding, with long-standing and emerging peacebuilding organizations, including many faith-based ones, and we published a book by that same name, which helped open the field to important new tools, like Appreciative Inquiry. We designed and facilitated an array of trainings to put our ideas into practice, inside and outside our denomination.

PDI was my first experience of collective spiritual exploration—of listening inward together with others in order to serve a stronger outward collective action. That taught me foundational lessons about building and working in spiritual community. My own faith practice had been largely internal, a resource for supporting myself and my work. PDI opened new paths for inviting and seeing the sacred in every dimension of my peacebuilding practice. *Being* in sacred community together, as we were, meant understanding that the ideas calling us were larger than any of us individually, or even denominationally. We let those ideas guide us, individually and collectively, and we developed practices for truing to them—practices of leaning into, listening for, and working *from* those ideas.

PDI was also one expression of a question I had long held: What would a *collective* healing practice look like? As a Christian Scientist, I had been steeped in the practice of healing prayer, turning to it my whole life for both my spiritual growth and my physical health. My practice was largely supported by individuals, called Christian Science practitioners, working with other individuals, like me. Christian Science practitioners pray with and for their patients, offering spiritual "treatment" to address any need— whether pertaining to physical health or finances, emotional turmoil or relationship challenges. Practitioners work to ground and deepen patients' understanding and experience of God's presence and power, often by sharing metaphysical ideas to strengthen patients' own prayers and by applying these ideas in prayer for whatever problem was brought to them for healing.

The first time I remember calling a practitioner myself was when I was eight and wracked with anxiety over some problems at school that felt, then, like the end of the world. What I most remember from that call is how respected I felt talking with her. She refused to see me as a problem, or even as someone having a problem. She listened lovingly to all my fears, and I felt as if they were gently and tenderly lifted off me, one by one. I carried back to school a tangible sense of the presence of a divine Love, in all circumstances, and my fears disappeared. A more adult iteration of that healing came in college when, facing deadlines and big exams, I came down with a whopper of a flu. I made a similar call to another practitioner and poured out my tale of woe. I vividly remember her first words: "Well, you can look forward to how God is going to handle it." Her simple, faith-grounded statement felt like warm sun dissipating a thick fog. It wasn't about what *I* needed to figure out or do; there was a bigger whole holding me, one that I could trust in and yield to. By the next day, I felt fine, and I moved graciously through all my work.

What would it mean to bring these lessons—not only the faith that grounded them but also their embodied experience—to the world of peacebuilding? Were there more resources available for healing the *social* body than I had yet encountered or learned how to mobilize? Did my own lived experience and spiritual deepening have more to teach me, and the world, about what peacebuilding can be?

The periphery becomes the center

I carried these questions with me to my church in Alton, hoping to find wisdom from my own learning to help address the conflict wrenching our congregation apart: the church's position on homosexuality. Our congregation was challenged to consider whether the Christian values we committed to as a community included acceptance of relationships outside of the heterosexual norm that was dominant, even in secular spaces, at that time. The ensuing conversation was difficult and divisive; people began to attack each other, sometimes publicly but more often behind-the-scenes, in language none of us, I thought, would ever use face-to-face. Positions hardened; friendships ended. Clearly, we were not equipped to handle this issue openly, honestly, and with mutual respect.

I held a clear conviction that my church was meant to be a place of healing, and I loved my church and its members. I also had a bent toward activism and a strong sense of how things should be done, supported by years of education to identify a "problem" I was well-trained to "solve." And my own prayers had directed me to be open to opportunities to build peace right where I was. So here was my chance.

But then I was elected Second Reader. In a Christian Science church, Readers are elected by the congregation to conduct the services. As a lay church, there are no clergy, and Readers do not "lead" in the traditional sense of the word. Instead, they follow a denomination-wide order of service, reading the weekly Bible lesson out loud on Sunday as the "sermon." The spiritual ideas from the scriptures themselves are meant to lead, and the denomination's guiding text on the role of Readers includes a prescription against direct leadership. I interpreted that to mean I needed to step back from any kind of activist role in addressing the conflict at hand. I trusted this direction, even though, to my activist sensibilities, it felt like inaction. Could *not doing* be the thing I was actually supposed to be *doing*?

I worked instead to support the church spiritually, thinking especially about the larger whole that held us. This larger whole was the deeper idea and ideal of church that I felt had been overrun and distorted by the conflict and how we'd handled it. Mary Baker Eddy, the founder of Christian Science, defined church spiritually as, in part, "the structure of Truth and Love; whatever rests upon and proceeds from divine Principle." I studied and prayed with that ideal, asking myself what it meant to embody and inhabit *that* church, and how I, and we, might do so more fully—right where we were, in the middle of all the messiness and pain.

As I prayed with this spiritual definition of church as "the structure of Truth and Love," that little word "and" practically jumped off the page to me. It struck me that our church was hardening into two oppositional camps, both framing the conflict as truth *versus* love, each hitting the other over the head with their respective virtue. It became obvious that the real problem wasn't figuring out *which* one to choose but rather the assumption that they were oppositional—the idea that we had to choose between them at all. Church, as Eddy conceived it, was by definition the structure of Truth *and* Love. (When capitalized, both are seen as distinct synonyms for God.)

And *that* was the space I committed to inhabiting—the place structured by both Truth and Love. I trusted that this spiritual idea had drawn all of us to this church in the first place, and I held to that idea in thought and prayer. I spoke from that understanding in our church meetings and in my individual conversations with members, and I actively trusted that we could embody it together. This spiritual deepening, and the patient faith, insight, humility, courage, and affection it helped me express, was the kind of development my peacebuilder self most needed. That insight I'd had in my morning prayer the year before was helping me hold space for these values, inside myself and in community with my congregation.

Our church process moved forward more positively once we realized that the problem wasn't the issue itself but the way we were engaging it, and that we were letting it pull us away from our purpose. Things didn't resolve instantly or painlessly; it was often messy and uncomfortable work. But we became more humble and more self-aware. In the end, we focused on our collective commitment to embodying the values of Christian community, which we acknowledged was a living process that required ongoing conversations about all sorts of difficult issues. We committed to embodying our highest values in how we had those conversations, trusting those values to guide us in our way forward.

Being clear on *how* we wanted to be together awakened and strengthened us for *what we wanted to do* together, and we stepped into a much more active and engaged presence in the community as a result. That work pulled us all forward, together.

It also gave me embodied learning of how spiritual ideas and ideals can hold space around a conflict and open the potential for transformation for the community and the people in it, including myself. With all my academic attention to mobilizing religious resources for peace "out there," the conflict in my church gave me the experience of strengthening my own religious resources in my own community. Focusing inward had ultimately prepared our church for its renewed focus outward with new strength and clarity of purpose.

The same was true for me. As our church stepped into a more outward-facing engagement, so, too, did my peacebuilding practice. In the fall of 2002, my father and I hosted a Middle East peace conference. Perhaps our years of vigorous but respectful disagreements had larger political significance?!

My dad had become more politically active later in life, raising money for Republican candidates for office at local, state, and national levels. He was a national finance chair for George W. Bush during his presidential campaign, and then finance chair for the RNC. In Bush's second term, he was named US ambassador to Portugal.

My father was also a man of deep faith, and he had a rock-solid belief in the fundamental dignity and wholeness of every person. That belief allowed him to engage compassionately and respectfully with people very different from himself. It's part of what helped him move in circles of power, and aspiring power, in ways that easily won people's trust. He also had a well-honed faith in a larger, divine power, which he saw as wholly loving and good. These beliefs and commitments helped us transcend our differences and occasionally opened up new understanding around thorny issues.

So it was natural, as I continued my research and writing on religious resources for peace, to talk about these ideas with my dad. He had been on a transformational trip to Israel with then Governor Bush and maintained a strong interest in the region. During one of our impassioned conversations about mobilizing religion for peace in the Middle East, he said to me, "Well, I'm having dinner with the president next Tuesday. Can you write me some talking points?"

"Of course!" I blurted. I don't think I heard anything else he said for the rest of the conversation.

I asked Cynthia Sampson to help me brainstorm what to write, and she brought in her friend Marc Gopin, a rabbi who was involved with peacebuilding in Israel and Palestine and was teaching part-time at Fletcher. While nothing directly came of Dad's evening with the president, it furthered our conversation and my dad's interest in doing more to support peacemaking efforts in the Middle East. We began planning to bring grassroots peacebuilders from Israel and Palestine together with American policymakers from both political parties for a peace conference, and he happily offered his home on Clapboard Island, just off the coast of Maine, for the gathering.

"Middle East peace conference" sounds so lofty, and although part of me was sparked by that loftiness, I was most excited by having a space where so many different parts of me could work together in a way that felt like play. It was hard work, of course, and full of the risks of the new and unknown, but fun nevertheless. I also loved my dad, and it was a real joy to have something we could work on together in genuine partnership, in spite of our differences.

Dad and his wife, Dawn, had a beautiful and gracious home, and they used it often for entertaining, including high-level political fundraising. It was easy for me to be dismissive and cynical about this kind of entertaining and the resources it took to support it, spending that I judged as misdirected and wasteful. Yet it became obvious that this depth of experience made the conference possible, especially on short notice. My dad and Dawn had the supplies, the staff, the relationships with caterers and boat drivers, and the know-how to prepare accommodations where 25 people would sleep, eat, meet, and meander. And they were both genuinely thrilled to be able to contribute that in the service of this venture. I was humbled and grateful.

Preparing and tending the meeting space also took on other important dimensions. Because we were meeting over the Jewish Sabbath and our attendees included Orthodox Jews, there were many provisions we had to make to accommodate that: things like getting paper plates and disposable silverware for our guests that kept kosher; scheduling ferry and other travel times well before sundown on Friday; and finding Muslim or Christian participants willing to take notes for their Jewish fellow delegates during the

Sabbath. I remember walking around before folks arrived, taping bathroom light switches into the on position and pre-pulling toilet paper in the rooms where our Orthodox guests were staying.

Ironically, the parts of the retreat I remember least are the formal conversations and the agenda we created for those. It's not that I didn't think the content itself was important, but others were tending that aspect of the conference. I was focused on building a space to *hold* the whole—a space that included not only the issues we gathered to discuss but also the people themselves, and the larger potential. We had no delusions of trying to solve the Israeli-Palestinian conflict in our time together, but we did want to begin to build a bridge between grassroots activism and elite-level politics. Our facilitation team was skillful at creating a space for honest, difficult conversations and building stronger connections between people. But we also wanted to open space for vision and imagination, which are difficult to engage during the day-to-day press of conflict, and we wanted to invite religion and faith in positive ways, for all. I sensed we could build a much *bigger* space than any of us were used to inhabiting.

One night at dinner, I knew we'd succeeded in creating that bigger space. I sat with Orthodox Rabbi Menachem Froman, an Israeli settler and well-known peacemaker close to Palestinian religious leaders, and with Imam Yahya Hendi, the Muslim chaplain at Georgetown University. We talked about healing, in our faith traditions and in our individual experiences. Rabbi Froman shared that his wife, Hadassah, was studying healing with a Muslim Sufi teacher. When I talked about the work of Christian Science practitioners, Imam Hendi was intrigued and asked, "Could a Muslim be one of those?" I had to smile at the question. Here we were, with our different religious and life experiences, inhabiting together the deepest places of our own faiths. It all sparked a liveliness of spiritual imagination that even I hadn't anticipated.

I was able to draw upon my whole self for the Clapboard Island conference—not only upon my intellectual gifts but also upon my relational, spiritual, familial, aesthetic, activist, and managerial knowledge and skills. In so doing, I saw that I was drawn to tending the space that held the issues and the people as much as, if not more than, the issues themselves. The satisfaction I felt pointed me to clearer channels for my unfolding peacebuilding work. As much as there was a need for bringing people together across ethnic, religious, or other relational latitudes, there was also a compelling need for bringing together "levels" and sectors—from those working most locally to those working nationally, often in government, and internationally, as global policymakers and funders. That was a kind of vertical integration—of gathering and building connections—often ignored in a field focused primarily on making peace between groups fighting across horizontal lines of difference. On Clapboard Island, I recognized my unique skills, interest, and experience in carving channels of connection between vertical layers, exemplified even in my own family, where my heart grounded me in the local and communal while my dad focused on the elite level.

How, exactly, I was meant to apply all of this felt less clear, but the need to think forward came quickly. Around the same time as the conference, I learned my dad was taking his company public, and the stock he had put in his children's names when we (and his company) were small was suddenly real, and very big. The next year, at age 37, I came into $20 million. I was shocked by the suddenness of it all, and I was anxious to be the best steward I could be of these unexpected—and unearned—resources.

Even through the anxiety, I interpreted the windfall as a sacred invitation to do the work I most wanted to do in the world, in the way I most deeply believed it should be done. I knew I wanted to help animate the full potential of ordinary people in the work of peace, but I also had no idea how or where to start. Having significant financial resources to live into my vision was literally beyond my wildest imaginings—and not at all my father's intention. He made clear that he wouldn't have consciously chosen to give his adult children this much money at this point in our lives, and he hardly concealed his fear that his hard work and good fortune would now turn us into lazy good-for-nothings. I was left with huge amounts of self-pressure, fear, uncertainty, guilt, and confusion. I felt just plain *overwhelmed*.

I incorporated Catalyst for Peace as a private foundation to hold my vision and my stock so that I could resource one with the other. I assumed that creating a space for the kind of integrative work I'd brought to the Clapboard Island conference would be my best focus, especially considering the relationships and access I could draw on. But my first attempts to do that with my new resources ended badly, in part from naively thinking I needed to do it all, and all at once. I also felt like others co-opted my good intentions for their own agendas, which was painful and made it hard to go forward. I would eventually receive the gifts of learning from these experiences, but at that time, I felt even more confused about how to use these resources in the world.

Once again, as had happened when I was nursing my baby during graduate school, my own life and experience yielded new insights and inspiration that guided me forward. The same year I came into that money, another long-held vision finally, after decades of work, became a reality: the Marcia P. Hoffman School of the Arts was christened in my childhood hometown of Clearwater, Florida, named in honor of my mother. The example embodied by this new arts school, and my mom's dedicated work on its behalf, turned out to hold important lessons and insights for my own work—and for the core values we would embed in Fambul Tok.

Social creativity

In the mid-1970s, my family moved from the Chicago area to Clearwater, Florida. At that time, Florida's Gulf Coast felt to my parents like a cultural backwater. They were huge believers in the life-changing value of the arts for individuals and for communities, and they jumped in to strengthen the region's foundational arts institutions. My mom became very active with the Florida Orchestra, and then she and my dad dedicated themselves over many years to building Ruth Eckerd Hall, a new, state-of-the-art performing arts center.

As an early teen, I saw the hard work it took to raise funds and build public support for the project, and I was constantly surprised that my parents had to host so many meetings over so many years with so many kinds of people, from civic leaders to corporate power brokers to individuals of wealth. My teenage self thought it was pretty cool to meet many of the stars of early events at the Hall, and to have people like Tony Randall and Kitty Carlisle over for dinner at our house before they hosted a major fundraiser. But I also absorbed and internalized deeper lessons about money, community, and social change. I saw that financial resources can be powerful when they are linked to long-term, strategic, community-building processes, and that something as difficult to define as "culture" can be core to community vitality.

Though Clearwater didn't lack wealth, the kind of active philanthropic culture that supported the arts in Chicago did not exist. My parents understood this to mean that people simply weren't as used to collectively directing their wealth to fund large philanthropic projects . . . yet. Their work was as much about building a community to support a vibrant arts culture as it was about building an arts center. As the philanthropic community in Clearwater grew, it mobilized more readily around other community ventures. When Ruth Eckerd Hall opened in 1983, the community was primed and ready to both enjoy it and continue to support it.

My mom's work didn't end there. She refocused her efforts, working tirelessly toward growing arts education programming until she passed on in 1994. By 2003, the work had grown exponentially, generating abundant community interest and support. There was a new, state-of-the-art classroom and performance facility to be named in her honor, and arts education programming was overflowing.

During the final planning stages for that facility, Kathy Rabon, the Hall's executive director, discovered an old document outlining a plan and strategic vision for arts education, written by my mom several years before she died. Sharing the document with my brother and me, Kathy noted with astonishment that, despite her death, virtually everything in my mom's long-term vision had come true. She had helped lay the foundation and establish the framework for the program's growth in powerful ways. And she had done it so deftly, always inviting and affirming of others' leadership, that the plan continued to unfold well after she was no longer around to tend it. She had reflected on what she wanted to see more of—lively creativity, individual and social imagination, and vibrant whole-community engagement—and then she embraced the process of inviting and expressing those qualities and ideas more fully in the present. She saw them, in some measure, as already there, just not yet awakened. And she acted accordingly. Today, the Marcia P. Hoffman School for the Arts reaches more than 45,000 students a year, offering them more than 80,000 hours of arts experiences.

This was the kind of work I wanted to be doing—not building an arts center but working in the way my mother had, building a home for the work I thought was most needed in the world, with vision, invitational presence, patience and persistence. I had learned, sometimes slowly and sometimes painfully, that trying to influence policymakers wasn't my calling. Doing so felt like beginning with the assumption that power is located *out there* (or *up* there). My vision was a people- and community-centered approach to peace, one that could be mobilized and magnified systemically and strategically—a vision that invoked the same *already-not-yet* mindset my mom had used in her work. I interpreted this to mean being willing to live into, and to live out from, that vision over time, as I was continuously building it in the world.

Chapter 9

BRINGING MY WHOLE SELF

I n 2005, I was inspired and energized by John Paul Lederach's new book, *The Moral Imagination: The Art and Soul of Building Peace*. Peacebuilding, John Paul argued, should be defined as a creative act, one born from the "moral imagination" but grounded in the hard realities of life and conflict. The central question of this work, he wrote, is: "How do we transcend the cycles of violence that bewitch our human community while still living in them?"[5]

The Moral Imagination also resonated with my good friend and colleague Barbara Hartford, who sensed its unique fit with her organization. Barb was the director of peacebuilding at the United Religions Initiative (URI), a global grassroots interfaith organization that had partnered with PDI for the Positive Approaches

---

5   John Paul Lederach, *The Moral Imagination: The Art and Soul of Building Peace* (New York: Oxford University Press, 2005), 5.

to Peacebuilding conference, and she wanted to bring John Paul's approach into URI's programming. "Would you like to be a co-creator of this work with me?" she asked.

It was a delicious invitation, and one I couldn't resist. I flew to San Francisco to join Barb, John Paul, and John Paul's long-time collaborator Herm Weaver to brainstorm possibilities. Barb no doubt suspected I might consider funding whatever came out of these meetings, but I was still raw from my first "failures"; I had already experienced how often money distorts conversations, expectations, and relationships. It was important to me that my contributions to the conversation be received on their own merit. I didn't want my funder identity to be public.

After a lively morning of conversation, we broke for lunch and walked to the Warming Hut at the base of the Golden Gate Bridge. I walked alongside Herm, who asked, in a matter-of-fact voice, "So are you the funder?" My heart sped up with a jumble of surprise, fear, disappointment, and an unfamiliar glimmer of something I came to identify later as relief.

"My cover's blown, eh?" I said to Herm with a nervous smile.

Herm said that he didn't see any reason not to acknowledge it, and that it didn't add to or take away from the substance of my contribution (or anyone else's) in any way. I think my shoulders visibly lowered several inches, in that way in which you only realize how much tension you've been holding when you feel it fall away. His ease with the question helped me feel more fully present and more comfortable in my own skin.

Inside the Warming Hut, huddled around a café table, we did indeed feel warmed—by soup, laughter, and the singularly insightful reflections and questions John Paul fed back from the morning conversation. Then JP grabbed a napkin and started doodling a vision that was animating his imagination, a sort of layered, bubbly timeline. He explained that the circles and cycles he drew represented an ideal arc of a program, an iterative cycle of action and reflection over time. The arc encompassed not one training but several periodic sessions stretched out over a couple of years, say, with teams drawn from around the world, ready and perhaps relieved to take time away from frontline peace work for reflection and learning. Between these "training" sessions, the teams would continue their on-the-ground work, applying what they learned and generating new questions and insights to bring back to the next session. Periodically, the session facilitators would visit the teams, supporting them in their local contexts. This cyclical structure could create a kind of learning organism, not only enhancing the capacity and practice of the participants but also feeding into and strengthening the larger organization within which the learning organism was situated.

I felt my heart sparkle and sing. The learning journey we were imagining together was both individual and communal, inner and outer, and included *us* and a space for our own learning. It invited and centered internal, local leadership and resources and supported them over time with strong process and content. The layered, connected bubbles illuminated a framework encompassing all of those dimensions—a space where a person could bring all of herself.

The others also lit up with excitement. Barb and her colleagues said this was exactly what they wanted for URI, and John Paul said this kind of program could most help faith communities rise to their fullest peacebuilding capacity. By then, my heart was burning so strongly I could no longer stay silent. I gulped and said, "Well,

John Paul, if you'll design and run it, I'll commit to funding it!" I caught everyone by surprise, including myself, but off we went.

From the outset, I knew I didn't want to be a distant donor. But I worried that participating while also funding could lead to problems, and I wasn't sure how to navigate that tension. In an email, John Paul shared valuable perspective:

> It seems to me that the real issue is one of gift, voice, vocation if you will, combined with transparency and honesty. One of the ways I think about this is in reference to a healthy system or community and I think it requires embracing a paradox in reference to funders: How to accompany and create healthy boundaries.

He illuminated a vision of the peacebuilding system in which a funder wasn't separate from the system but part of it. Each element of his email illuminated pathways through the funder/practitioner dilemma, ways that felt deep and true to me. "Gift, voice, [and] vocation" guide participation, not external criteria like money, formal education, and job title. "Transparency" and "honesty" are qualities of character and *ways* of working, not simply facilitative tools or techniques. "How to accompany and create healthy boundaries" describes a living tension that invites practice and ongoing discernment, as well as courageous self-knowledge. It does not lay out an externally derived, rule-based decision-making matrix, and it does not imply a point at which the tension is ever "solved." And each dimension he referenced clearly applied to *every* part of the system, not just to the funder—an integrity of the whole that felt so fully right. For the first time, I began to envision a role as a funder that felt like a learning adventure, one that called forth the parts of me I most yearned to bring and allowed me to play an active, integrative role rather than merely offer external financial support for work done by others.

John Paul shared more about what he meant by "accompaniment," and his words became a beacon, guiding my movement through new and unfamiliar waters with the URI initiative and beyond. He wrote:

> Accompaniment as a philosophy and discipline is what I call "an alongsideness"—in practical terms for the funder this means a participation with respect just as any other participant has, knowing that anyone of us had good ideas, particular skills and insights, but that no one of us has it all. In the case of the funder it means that ideas/insights/skills are made available and present but are not tied to influence of the money, as in "my opinion counts more because I am funding." . . . What I refer to is something more organic: Accompaniment requires becoming an equal voice on the basis of context, process and interaction on the terms set out by those involved.

I understood John Paul's idea of "becoming an equal voice on the basis of context, process and interaction on the terms set out by those involved" as a way into co-creation, an approach I felt called to and that brought out my best. Not coincidentally, it was also the approach I found most fun. The vision and sensibility John Paul outlined opened a larger space for me than I had been able to find myself.

The journey from the vision JP sketched on a napkin to the reality of the Moral Imagination in Interreligious Peacebuilding program took over a year, but in December of 2006, just more than 20 peacebuilders from all around the world gathered at the Ralston White Retreat house in Mill Valley, north of San Francisco. The heart-shaped lawn in front of the main house welcomed us all warmly to the beautiful property, originally a wedding gift from White to his bride in 1910 and named by him the "Garden of Allah."

We had teams of interfaith peacebuilders from southern India, Ethiopia, northern Uganda, and the Philippines—Muslims, Hindus, and Christians of all stripes; clergy and laypeople; experienced practitioners and students; organizational leaders and community mobilizers. We also had an organizational learning and planning team, mostly US-based, to support the whole and harvest the learnings from the two-year program. Our fatigue, our excitement, our nerves, our dreams, our uncertainty—all were present as we gathered for the first time. Herm chose to open our gathering, as he would often do, with a song he had written called "Who Am I?" He said his first version of the song was all about what he did. But now he sang about the gentle perils of asking that question—of the fears and self-consciousness it can bring up. What if I'm not good enough? What if I'm wrong? What if they don't like me? And then his own simple answer: "I am my father's son, and my son's father," he sang.

His opening acknowledged our anxieties, and we were each invited to be present in, and as, our own hearts, first and foremost. It's funny how sometimes just acknowledging the uneasiness allows you to move on and move in—into a fuller presence. It certainly did for me.

As the evening wore on, my own insecurities started to creep back in, accompanied by my world-class capacity for self-pressure. As I listened to the introductions, I felt like I was "the one not like all the others." I was neither a facilitator nor on a country team nor part of URI's staff. I was, in part, the funder, and I was still uncomfortable being seen that way. I knew I most wanted to bring a settled, light, expectant, supportive energy—my stock-in-trade, most of the time. But I felt increasingly unable to do that—which, of course, made me feel even more pressured.

Once again, the spirit of the space asserted itself and held me with more grace than I could hold myself. Charles Gibbs, URI's executive director and an Episcopal priest, shared a quote he carried with him, attributed to an anonymous Methodist missionary: "The first thing I do when I go into a new place is to take off my shoes to remind myself that I am standing on holy ground. Otherwise, I might make the mistake of believing that I bring God with me." Ahhhhhh. I felt the weight, once again, lifting off my shoulders, and with that sensation came a realization of how imaginary that weight had actually been. All I had to do was take off my shoes to be able to feel the holy ground already right there under my feet.

The country teams prepared presentations for the whole group, giving overviews of their settings, challenges, and hopes. I was on the organizational learning team, whose members would each support a country team for this activity. I joined the team from Uganda, made up of senior leaders of the Acholi Religious Leaders Peace Initiative, or ARLPI, whose work and stories riveted me. Sister Mary Tarcisia Lakot was almost matter-of-fact when she introduced herself by saying, "My father and mother were killed in the war; my brother was killed . . ." I was incredibly moved by the dignity, courage, and humility with which they faced their circumstances. I felt like I was sitting at the feet of the masters, people with such extraordinary alignment of their inner ideals and outward actions, working in the most challenging circumstances imaginable.

In the course of our conversation, I asked what they felt was the biggest challenge to peace in their region. Without a moment's hesitation, Sheikh Musa Khalil answered, "The ICC."

"What?" I gasped.

"The International Criminal Court is a bigger obstacle to peace now than Joseph Kony or his rebels," he said.

I was shocked. I simply couldn't process that an *international justice mechanism*, for goodness' sake, could be more of an obstacle to peace than a notorious warlord and his Lord's Resistance Army (LRA), which had perpetrated so many atrocities.

He said that the Acholi religious leaders, among others, had been working for years to reach Kony and the LRA leaders and persuade them to negotiate a peace. Sheikh Khalil had been part of a small delegation of religious leaders who had recently trekked through the jungles of southern Sudan to find him. When they did, they had to persuade several rings of armed guards, one after the other, to let them pass. When they finally reached Kony, he indicated that he was willing to talk peace. Sheikh Khalil felt they had been making meaningful progress—until the International Criminal Court indicted Kony and four of his senior leaders. This caused the rebel leader to slink deeper into hiding, abruptly ending any further opportunity for dialogue and preempting the chance Sheikh Khalil had seen for progress toward lasting peace.

As they told me more about their work back home, the Ugandan team huddled as close to the crackling fire as they could, wrapped in borrowed coats and sweaters to fend off the chill of Northern California's nighttime fog. They explained that the Acholi wanted to use their traditional ways of dealing with conflict, the cultural and communal values they rested upon, such as forgiveness, to build a path toward peace and reconciliation. Sheikh Khalil said the international community's assumption that justice was found in prosecution undermined the Acholi's ability to advocate for and engage in a broader reconciliation process. They were convinced that an Acholi forgiveness process would draw Kony out of hiding and into a peace agreement. The Acholi religious leaders worked toward this vision on both the community and national levels. They had become trusted intermediaries for the national government and for the rebels, and they were—or at least, they had been—uniquely positioned to be able to reach the rebel commanders, literally and figuratively.

Sheikh Khalil and his team expanded and enriched my understanding of justice by centering local healing and reconciliation practices, unacknowledged and untapped by the international system. The framework of formal justice, meanwhile, had a totalizing effect, erasing the Acholi culture's communal and restorative approaches from the global conversation and simultaneously undermining their local power and efficacy. There was no policy or organizational infrastructure that invited and supported culturally rooted approaches at the national or international level.

The ARLPI team shared stories about reviving traditional communal ceremonies to help reintegrate former child soldiers into their communities. As I listened, I understood that the Acholi culture and community offered something important, not just for peace in northern Uganda but for the world. We all could learn something valuable—and much needed—from their communal, restorative approach, if it was given space and support to work and grow.

Curiosity shows up for me as questions, and new questions began to form in my thought: What would it take to center and support that kind of culturally rooted approach internationally? What would it be like if postwar justice mechanisms proactively valued existing cultural resources? What could be possible then?

At the end of the week, John Paul invited the country teams to imagine what they might tell their grandchildren one day about how their work had helped their homelands. He asked us to begin by saying, "Everything in this story is true, except for the things that haven't happened yet . . ."

While the country teams worked together, the members of the organizational learning team wrote their own companion visions for the team they had accompanied earlier. I had seen the depth of resource and capacity in the ARLPI team and in the organization, community, and culture they represented. I had also sensed the brokenness of the external global systems within which they were operating. I could imagine the impact that their values, when actualized, could have on the world—if and when the world could find a willingness to learn from them. And all of that shaped the vision I outlined and read to the group when it was my turn.

The effect was like a mirror, reflecting back to the Acholi the substance of their work and the power and potential of their values and approach. It was obvious from their smiles and the animated conversation that followed how inspiring and affirming this mirroring was for them. And they weren't the only team with this experience. Across the board, the visions shared by the organizational learning team were more vibrant than what the teams articulated themselves. That the organizational team had the capacity to express this fullness of vision makes some sense: when you daily face every imaginable obstacle to your work, sustaining a systems-level vision of embodied positive transformation is difficult, if not impossible. As I reflected on the reality of that contrast, it did not strike me as a weakness of fieldwork but rather as an illumination of an important role outsiders can play, of how the presence of an outsider can be critical to creating space that allows for the kind of grounded transcendence John Paul described.

It may be a luxury of the outsider to help spark the imagination that catalyzes renewed wholeness and creative potential. If so, that luxury isn't something to be ignored or avoided. It is something that must be intentionally built in and on. Our meeting illuminated that moral imagination is not just an individual accomplishment. It is and can be—must be—a communal enterprise.

The Acholi religious leaders' wisdom opened a vision in me, and that vision became like a lighthouse in the distance, a tiny, faraway light that nevertheless illuminated a new path forward. I imagined the international community recognizing success in an indigenous justice model like the one ARLPI promoted, and then restructuring the ICC and other international instruments to integrate traditional, community-based ways of reconciliation. This vision, in turn, shaped and informed *my* vision of an international system—one that centered itself in *invitation* and *support*, and in which cultural and communal riches could ground the approach to justice and peace.

As it turned out, it would not be in Uganda but on the other side of the continent, in Sierra Leone, where I would live out that vision. Eight months later, when I would meet John Caulker for the first time, I was primed and ready to help bring a new approach from vision to reality, to create space for local culture, customs, and community to lead the way—and to want to share what they were doing with the world.

Part III

BUILDING A HOME FOR THE WORK

Chapter 10

THE IDEAS WE REST UNDER

My dad was a homebuilder. A land developer, actually: he built whole communities, full of *lots* of homes. It was his success as a homebuilder that funded Catalyst for Peace—so "home" is literally the foundation for my work as a peacebuilder.

My mom was a home*maker*. Besides creating spaces of beauty and comfort in our physical homes, she worked hard to create a household that supported us to grow into the best versions of ourselves. This work ranged from quotidian acts of care and feeding to the most expansive spiritual development she knew how to offer. Home was the deeply rooted, eminently practical space that supported my being and becoming.

I had the incredible privilege of growing up in some of the most amazing homes you can imagine. Together, my parents ensured we inhabited these spaces generously, teaching us extravagant hospitality. Our doors were always open to family, friends, and the community. We were the go-to place for class parties and church events and the site of regular raucous gatherings of friends-who-felt-like-family. We hosted annual fundraisers for the community organizations my parents were most committed to. We had a revolving door of people living with us when they were in between places or in a moment of need. Friends and family were always welcome to come for their vacations. Learning to cook meant learning to cook for crowds. I can plan, shop, and cook for 20 people for a week without batting an eye.

I learned that *home* was more than a private space of retreat; it was something that could be built out into the world to create meaningful spaces of belonging and becoming for others. I expanded the concept of building home and building community into a channel for my activist and creative energies, work that was bound together with deep relational commitments. This kind of engagement of *home* draws on both the homebuilding and the homemaking energies of each of my parents, weaving together the practical, the spiritual, the philanthropic, and the entrepreneurial.

When I started Catalyst for Peace, I had yet to find a home for the way I felt called to work in the world; a community that braided together peacebuilding, spirituality, and money into a larger whole. From the beginning, part of my commitment was to live that home into being and expression—building and inhabiting it—as I went. I wasn't totally sure what that meant, at least not in a way that I could verbalize. But my core commitment was not only to supporting the work I thought the world most needed but also to being and bringing my whole self and to working as fully as possible in the way I thought we were *meant* to work in the world. Building

Catalyst for Peace as the home for this work is both the most global and the most personal way I've inhabited the idea of peacebuilding as homebuilding.

Throughout the emergence and growth of Fambul Tok, I held this question: *What is the home for this way of working in the world?* I wanted this home to have a foundation of mutually enlivening and equitable relationships—between programming and the people it is enacted for, between an outside donor and a national program leader, between Global North and South, between white and black. Building these individual relationships—and both John and I owning that our own roles would be redefined as we did so—was consciously part of building a home for this way of working in the world. And because there was not yet a national or international support structure—a home—for working that way, we had to build it ourselves, as we worked. Sort of like a snail. Or a turtle.

What space, though, do you inhabit when you are still in process, when you are building the home for the work as you're doing it? Of course, John and I had organizational homes, in Catalyst for Peace and Fambul Tok, and we were both tending to organizational development. But that's not what I mean, exactly. The poet Rilke exhorts us to "live the questions," rather than assume that the purpose of a question is always to find an answer. I hear that, in part, as telling us to live *in* the questions, as if a question is spacious, like a place of habitation. I find ideas to be like that as well. Ideas can open up gracious spaces for us to sink into, to take up residence in, to gather around, to lean into, to just . . . be. Like a park pavilion or the branches of a giant mango tree on a hot day, ideas can offer open air for refuge and reflection, even as life flows freely around and through.

The ultimate home for this work has been the core ideas, visions, and values we rest under. Three of these especially ground and shape our work, forming the spiritual architecture of the space we inhabit.

The first of these ideas we rest under is that *the answers are there*—the assumption and conviction that people and communities, even after war and violence or in the midst of poverty or plague, have within them resources for, and answers to, the problems they are facing. From this perspective, the role of an outside supporter—whether it be an NGO, a local or national government, or an international donor—is not to go in to fix or "save" but rather to look for, notice, encourage, magnify, and build on the resources that are already within the community itself. This is at the heart of what it means to build peace *from the inside out.*

A second idea we lean into is that *we are in service of something much larger than ourselves*—and that we can trust this larger wisdom to guide us and our work. John and I have taken to calling this "the Bigger Hand." By committing to the larger wisdom that holds us and cultivating our receptivity to it, we open ourselves up to experiencing that wisdom more fully, which can—and as we have seen, often does—open up new and unexpected resources for our work.

The third core idea we inhabit is that *real power is in lived goodness*—in the capacity to build, not destroy; the capacity to create and co-create, to imagine and to do, that which is good for the whole. "Lived goodness" is the active expression of the belief that people are inherently good, and want to *do* good, but circumstances often make it hard for us to act from that goodness. This is the opposite, in fact the renunciation of, the Hobbesian worldview that humans in their natural state are inherently selfish, solitary, warring brutes, a worldview that underpins the international system I was taught. Working from this different assumption consciously invites the best of ourselves and of others into expression and action—it invites us to live from and into our goodness, together. That, in turn, activates real, sustainable power. It is both generative and regenerative, and worthy of every measure of support.

These ideas may at first sound abstract, unwieldy, or impractical. Yet they have been solid, generative, and constant sources of support and direction throughout the years that John and I have worked together. And they have had practical, programmatic, and technical expressions, from the local to the national and global levels of our work. In fact, the movement from the conceptual to the technical, the flow from the universal to the personal and back again—I would say that is our real work. It *is* the building of the home for the work. It *is* the inhabiting of that home. It *is* the work of building peace—from the inside out.

In order to illuminate the home as we have been building it, my writing, too, flows between the 40-thousand-foot perspective and the close-up. I amplify not only the *what* but also the *how*, since it is often the how that holds the real substance and power of the work.

Embracing the unknown

In the early days of Fambul Tok, as volunteers were introducing the program to the first villages, it was clear that people everywhere were eager to engage the process. It was as if the invitation to community reconciliation were slaking a deep thirst. One volunteer saw personal opportunity in this excitement and told communities they would have to pay to participate, and then he pocketed the money.

I vividly remember John's distressed phone call to me on the day he discovered this. He was afraid it was just the kind of thing that could undermine Fambul Tok's credibility with the communities at these critical early stages.

I was devastated at the thought that someone had abused the trust of the community in this way, and I felt violated that he had done so in Fambul Tok's name. "How are you going to handle it?" I asked John, with genuine curiosity. I had no idea myself how best to respond to something like this, and I felt some of my familiar, anxiety-rooted pressure building up again. I needed him to have a solution.

"I don't know," John said after a short silence. "But together we will figure a way out."

My shoulders dropped. I intuitively sensed the truth of the statement and immediately felt the release that came along with it. I let out a heavy sigh.

John was right. Together with the local Fambul Tok staff, he gathered the communities the volunteer had stolen from, explained the situation, and facilitated a discussion on how to deal with it. The community leaders believed that, given the scope of the violation, this was actually a matter for the police, who subsequently arrested the man. The conversation about the problem ended up strengthening the community fabric in the very ways the *fambul tok* process as a whole was intended to do. It strengthened Fambul Tok as well, and the transparent process of consultation helped protect Fambul Tok's reputation for trustworthiness.

John's response encapsulates one of the biggest lessons I've learned from him and from working with Fambul Tok: *Together we will figure a way out.* John knew from his own experience that there is wisdom in the community, a trustworthy, collective, available wisdom, a wisdom greater than individual problem-solving skills. He was devoting his life to supporting Sierra Leone's rural communities in rediscovering their core, animating wisdom and tapping into it to address their wounds. And in this moment, he was able to lean into that power himself, that greater wisdom—the very power he was dedicated to nurturing.

John's statement illustrates the larger pattern of Fambul Tok's approach, as well as the broader lesson he and I came to see and experience repeatedly. When we are intentionally serving the greater good—listening for and trusting in the active presence of that which is good for the whole—we can trust that power to guide us, right where we are. Problem-solving doesn't fall on any one of us alone. And in fact, when we are willing to put aside the ego gratification of thinking we have all the answers and instead come together to trust this wisdom of the whole, we are much more likely to discover effective ideas.

I recognize there was a part of me that really did want John to have an answer right away, largely to soothe my own anxiety. I was investing a great deal in his leadership of this nascent, first-of-its-kind program. But John wasn't abdicating his responsibility or his leadership by not coming up with an answer himself; he was actually exercising it more fully. Turning to the community was an embodied expression of seeing and treating them as equal partners in program development and implementation—as intellectual and moral equals who were not simply capable of handling the situation but were the very people who *should* do so, because they really *were* in ownership of their community. He was rejecting the pressure to demonstrate full "expertise" as an individual leader and instead trusting in the larger community wisdom. Admitting we don't have an answer ourselves—and don't need to—is one key to inviting others' knowledge and to accessing communal wisdom, especially when accompanied by a sincere willingness to go forward anyway, together.

Yet I frequently experience a pull to demonstrate my expertise and problem-solve on my own, an urge stemming from internalized cultural assumptions that equate competence with having all the answers. This pull, familiar to those of us from Western schools of conditioning, can blind us, keeping us from looking for, recognizing, and therefore accessing so much greater, readily available wisdom.

The outsider-as-expert dynamic has even been internalized by the very communities we want to help, illustrating the systemic nature of the challenge. When Fambul Tok first began work in Kono, a local political leader recited to us all the problems people in the district were facing, a tactic for convincing John and his staff to work there. Kono District, the center of Sierra Leone's diamond industry, contains pockets of extreme wealth and great swaths of extreme poverty; it also saw some of the worst atrocities of the war. Everything in Kono is intensely politicized, and these characteristics have made it the object of national and global attention. That, in turn, meant the Fambul Tok staff faced an especially entrenched version of what they describe as "NGO mentality," a learned dependence on outsiders for assistance. This dependence comes with an assumption that assistance is money, which only outsiders have, and that money is secured by articulating need in ever more compelling ways. More subtle, but in my view more problematic, is the way "NGO mentality" diminishes people's and communities' own resources, a learned helplessness that has been internalized over time and makes it difficult for communities to see, value, or mobilize their own capacities and potential.

The humanitarian aid industry perpetuates this outside-in dynamic. Very few international or even national NGOs in Sierra Leone have active, ongoing, district-based presences; most are based in Freetown. With headquarters in global capitals like London, New York, and Geneva, these organizations define the problems "out there" in their own terms, often before they've even been to the places where they intend to work. They then determine and design solutions, usually based on their own expertise or on their organization's purpose, and they impose those solutions de facto on communities. They're able to work this way because they have the financial resources, and they own the definition, design, and decision-making processes. In international work, there is increasing use of language like "consulting" locals, "fostering" full "participation," "inclusiveness," and even "community ownership." But the reality of what is experienced by communities is rarely any of those things; and in fact, "consultation" is often yet another outsider-defined activity serving an outsider-defined purpose, pulling locals further away from their own agendas and agency in the service of someone else's. This whole system increases disaffection and disempowerment and further frays community fabric, even if it intends to do the opposite. This kind of "outside-in" approach assumes a separation of resources and expertise from the places and people with problems and needs, allowing only for a one-way flow of resources and expertise—from the outside in.

After listening to the Kono District leader's long list of challenges, John redirected the conversation. "We don't solve problems,"

John told him. "We create space." He explained Fambul Tok's core belief, one of the pillars of our work: *the answers are there*. Local communities already have a lot of resources, including the capacity to address many of their challenges, and they can begin with the resources they already have—especially if they come together. John explained to the Kono leader that Fambul Tok wasn't there to give money but to create space for communities to come together and solve their *own* problems. The message needed constant repetition, in virtually every new community where Fambul Tok worked, but it also tapped into and opened up a wellspring of energy for community leadership.

Creating space in this way—the *process* work of community mobilization and education—is much less visible than, say, building a health center or school or digging a well. It requires a reconceptualization of program deliverables, an ability to understand process *as* product, and a reorientation of program design. Engaging process means looking and listening for what is happening on the ground and then adapting programming to it in an ongoing way. This not only makes for better programming but also strengthens and sustains community creativity and collaboration, which in turn helps local leaders solve problems.

In real life, learning is cyclical, and cycles of action and reflection support organic growth—of people, of communities, and also of programming and organizations. We came to see that program planning needed to be cyclical and emergent, too, in order to honor and build on embodied, real-life learning. And that's not always easy, neither on a programming level nor on a personal one. Though I love and value learning, I often battle a great deal of self-pressure when I encounter the edges of my own knowledge and experience. In my role as a leader, I've worked to cultivate a companion impulse—a willingness to open to wisdom greater than my own. And it is in this opening out that I have come to see how *not knowing* can actually be a generative resource, for me personally and for the work I'm leading. Fambul Tok has taught me a great deal about how to be comfortable in not knowing, and it has shown me that "wisdom greater than my own" can come in and through and with other people, in community—and that this is something that can and should be intentionally cultivated.

Stepping back to step forward

Six months into the Fambul Tok program, it took every bit of pressure I could comfortably (and sometimes uncomfortably) assert to get John to take a break. Getting him and some of his key leadership team to leave Sierra Leone for a weeklong retreat in Vermont was like trying to stop an express train. The first several ceremonies had been wildly successful, and more and more communities were asking to participate. Begging, even. John had been dreaming of running just such a program at the community level for years, and he finally had an open canvas on which to paint that vision into reality. Fambul Tok was poised to roll out in several districts, and now that it was finally going, John didn't want to stop for anything or anyone.

But after the intensity of piloting the program, I knew that going forward sustainably required . . . stopping. At least briefly. Beyond the personal restorative value of taking a break, I also wanted to harvest the learning from the pilot before rolling out the program further. More pointedly, I wanted to put the same process values of

Fambul Tok's community work into operation at an organizational level. The staff was asking communities what they wanted, trying things out, and listening for what was working (or not) and what needed to come next; I felt we needed space to do the same thing, organizationally and in connection with program design.

Pausing and reflecting creates important internal space for learning. It honors and invites the wisdom latent in lived experience. It allows us time to reground our efforts in vision and purpose, which in turn prepares the ground for new creativity. After these critical first months of program implementation, we also had some practical organizational needs to tend, work best done in person. Though we needed a plan for building out Fambul Tok nationally, I felt the planning had to emerge "from within," meaning from an *embodied knowing and sensing* more than an abstract or intellectualized planning process. I saw a role for Catalyst for Peace in holding space for the cyclical learning process of real life, for the program as a whole—inviting the national leadership together with the global support team to reflect back and then listen forward together. So in the summer of 2008, we spent a week at the glorious Teal Farm in Huntington, Vermont, to move further through this learning cycle.

When it came time to build the plan for the rest of the year and beyond, our first attempt, rooted in an intellectual sense of what we "should" do next, felt dry and lifeless—burdensome, even. Yet John and his colleague Robert Roche, who had been leading the work on the ground, had cultivated an internalized understanding of the community mobilization process that supported true local ownership and successful community healing. So I invited them to walk us through every step of their process, starting with the moment Fambul Tok arrived in a new district. Listening carefully, I wrote everything out on our paper-covered tabletop, step by step, drawing lines and arrows to show how one thing connected and led to another and another. As we went, we talked through the nitty-gritty of what each step required of personnel, time, and resources. The result was a lovely, organic map of the delightfully nonlinear process of reawakening community wholeness and healing in Sierra Leone. Now, after our collective reflection, we could all see and name that process in specific detail; we had all internalized it.

"This is solid gold," I exclaimed, looking at the finished diagram.

We distilled this rough chart into a diagram that became a central part of Fambul Tok's training program and our publications. The chart was a critical tool for planning the next phase of program growth, including understanding, assessing, and realistically planning for the resources that would be needed, so we could make more accurate and effective decisions about program direction. We were now able to engage in that more detailed planning with grounded confidence and collective discernment.

With this action-reflection process, we were not "producing" a plan and a program, as if they were something disconnected from the organic wisdom of our collective experience. We were *growing* them. John and his team were asking, and the communities in Sierra Leone were telling them, what they needed to be whole again, after what they had suffered in the war. Catalyst for Peace was asking, and the Fambul Tok staff was telling us, what was needed in order to create the space for that to happen. Having distilled that embodied knowledge, the leadership team asked together in Vermont what would be needed organizationally to support and grow the work going forward. With all of those dimensions in place, we were able to envision and create a multilevel plan for helping that to happen.

THE **FAMBUL TOK**

IT ALL BEGINS WITH
CONSULTATION
(identify stakeholders)

1

DISTRICT
COORDINATOR
AND 2 ASSISTANTS

DISTRICT STAFF

RECRUIT

2

VOLUNTEERS

A DISTRICT EXECUTIVE,
AND CHAIRMAN
AND CHAIRLADY

HOLD
ONE WEEK
TRAINING

3

TOGETHER, STAFF AND EXECUTIVE
IDENTIFY COMMUNITIES

4

PREPARE FOR
BONFIRE

Hold sectional stakeholder meetings

Communities appoint Outreach Committee; Reconciliation Committee

Train OCs and RCs
THEY SENSITIZE COMMUNITIES
THEY ASSIST IN PREPARING FOR...

Bonfire

Cleansing Ceremony

PROCESS IN A DISTRICT

CONVENE ONGOING
LEARNING AND
REFLECTION

MONTHLY STAFF MEETINGS

SEMI-ANNUAL LEARNING/
SHARING/PLANNING MEETINGS

7

REPEAT
WHOLE CYCLE
IN NEW DISTRICTS

6

REPEAT
IN NEW SECTIONS

5

FOLLOW-UP
ACTIVITIES

**Community meetings
to determine
follow-up activities**

**Ongoing visitation
to communities**

FOOTBALL FOR
RECONCILIATION

PEACE TREES

RADIO LISTENING CLUBS

PEACE MOTHERS GROUPS

FAMBUL TOK
COMMUNITY FARMS

STUDENT PEACE CLUBS

We accomplished many important things that week, and it became clear that this reflection time was critical for strengthening the individual, relational, and organizational infrastructure it takes to do good work on the ground. From that point forward, we embedded the process of stepping back and reflecting together as a key part of the program's development. In fact, we treated pausing and reflecting *as* our work—an important part of it, anyway. Catalyst convened spaces like this inside and outside Sierra Leone, sometimes with a smaller leadership group and sometimes with the whole staff. The national staff also began a practice of gathering monthly for two to three days, in a different region each time, a practice we valued by including it in the program plan and budget, even when resources were tight. These became key spaces of mutual learning, creative collective problem-solving, and cross-pollination that rapidly spread new ideas across all the districts. The meetings also eased feelings of staff isolation or burnout. We even added the monthly and yearly meetings to our How It Works chart, recognizing how important these times were to the ongoing growth and development of the program itself.

Meetings like these were like an organizational wombing space—a delightfully alive, whole-body, organic space that supports the strengthening of the body of the work (both program and organization) until it can grow into the next level of its expression. Our Vermont wombing space, and others that followed, allowed for organic growth, unfolding, and emergence—of us as leaders, of the program, and of the organization(s) supporting it. They allowed us to inhabit our in-process-ness. Just as we needed to reconceptualize deliverables at the community level—seeing process *as* product and structuring programming around that—we needed to do the same at the national level, too. And doing so was a critical piece in the building of the home for this work.

Emergent design

In more technical language, these meetings were the heart of what I came to call our *learning and emergent design platform*. When the central intention of your work is to create space for communities to lead their own peace and development, it is impossible to predict exactly what will unfold too far in advance, and so we cultivated a practice of *emergent design*. With emergent design, the vision, approach, and principles of the work are solid and in place in advance, but the programming and process allow for flexibility to support learning in and adapting to unfolding circumstances. This approach supports organic, step-by-step growth, which we have found to be both more sustainable and more effective in laying the foundation for a broader, deeper transformation.

Organic growth, in turn, requires ongoing attention to what's emerging and what's needed next, and how best to activate that "next" in ways that are consistent with program goals and available resources. An "outside eye" supports this process, illuminating the big-picture perspective and helping to identify connections otherwise not easily visible, especially when you're in the thick of things on the ground. We structured time for attention, reflection, sensing, and discerning—together—by creating intentional learning spaces, which we call "learning circles." They represent perhaps the single most defining element of our inside-out approach. The regular retreats we held were emblematic of the learning circles embedded at every level of planning and implementation. Peace Mothers groups and Reconciliation Committees functioned as learning circles for local communities; the District Executives served this function for regional leaders; the national staff meetings and our organizational retreats did this at the national and global levels, respectively. By connecting the process of reflecting on lived experience and present circumstances with sensing, imagining, and planning forward, these groups and gatherings, taken together, became a platform for directing and redirecting action based on new learning and new circumstances.

Program design that supports—even honors—organic emergence is not the norm in most social change work, especially in the international peace and security context. Funding structures and practices are a big part of the problem. Funding for peacebuilding is often short-term and focused on discrete events or projects, with distinct predetermined (and limited) time frames. Funders typically require a detailed advance plan, with predetermined project timelines, goals, and outcomes. These demands make it difficult to work in long-term or emergent ways. The existing aid infrastructure assumes that "outcomes" are visible things, outward accomplishments, when so much of what really moves human lives is *interaction*—living process, in living relationships, over time.

Building funding and program spaces that honor living process and relationships is a critical need. It requires novel structures and practices, and it also requires explicit attention to the internal dimensions of the work—ways of being, knowing, and seeing. Learning happens in community, with trusted others, in trustworthy ongoing relationship, which requires a foundational commitment to the work of building and tending those relationships. Emergent design requires that we cultivate a willingness and capacity to be in the unknown and hold a radical trust in the process, which, of course, rests on having developed trustworthy processes in the first place. It also requires cultivating radical *self*-trust so that you can clearly discern and freely express your needs, questions, and ideas. Together, all of this opens up a more soul-centered approach to social change, for both the individual and the organization.

Car time

John and I have often joked that if Sierra Leone had had good roads, Fambul Tok wouldn't have become the program that it is. Because of Fambul Tok's commitment to its unique process, we spent hundreds of hours in the car together. Along the way, we discovered a kind of communication that turned out to be singularly generative.

I have typically traveled to Sierra Leone three or four times a year since Fambul Tok began, and with virtually all of the work centered in rural communities, stretching across six districts in each region of the country, that meant we spent a LOT of time on the road. I both loathed and loved the long drives over bumpy roads. I was awed by how unfazed the staff were by the travel. Their endurance and their capacity for doing hard things with apparent ease inspired and astonished me, and it continues to do so. I came to appreciate it as a sophisticated skill. The drives were physically challenging for me, and I was also impatient. If we had a community visit on the day's agenda, I thought the purpose of the drive was to *get there* so that the work of the day could commence. The fact that it could take hours (and hours . . .) to be able to begin the "purposeful" work of the day seemed to me inefficient at best. "Africa teaches you patience," my colleagues said. "Yeah, yeah—but when there's so much work to be done . . ." I would mutter to myself. My thinking evolved, however, as I came to recognize how fruitful those long expanses of unstructured time were, for both me and John as leaders and for the program itself. Those car rides actually became some of my most treasured and anticipated parts of any trip to Sierra Leone.

John is unique in NGO leadership in Sierra Leone in that he drives himself most of the time. (He finds it to be good "think" time and, in its own way, relaxing.) As one of his few peers with the full vision of the work and a grasp of project details at every level—programmatic, relational, organizational, values—I could join him in far-ranging conversation, zooming in and out from the big picture to minute details with seamless flow. It is a priceless gift to have uninterrupted conversation time with a partner, and especially one with John's heart, soul, intelligence, and leadership.

Car time became a time to process immediate challenges and a critical time for John to step back and reflect. The lengthy travels allowed for spontaneous reflection together on program development and emerging needs and opportunities, which naturally flowed into thinking through how to adapt program and organization accordingly. Doing this kind of planning wasn't premeditated. Without the pressures of needing to plan or problem-solve in predetermined chunks of time, and with a container of mutual trust and respect (enhanced by having so much unstructured time together), the questions, concerns, hopes, dreams, and visions all just naturally bubbled up. We circled around subjects in iterative ways, going up, down, and around an endlessly varied set of topics, interspersed with moments of silence, music, and conversation about our lives and families.

There was so much pressure, internal and external, to keep programming moving forward and growing. The demand from the people of Sierra Leone was huge, and the transformative results we witnessed only reinforced our desire to meet that demand. It took the road-enforced slowing down to resist that pressure in some measure. If not for these car rides, I don't think I ever could have asked for or claimed regular long spaces of unstructured conversation time with John, and I would venture to say he couldn't have asked it of me either. And yet the kind of co-creativity—not to mention relationship-building, soul nourishment, and fun—these hours opened up was unparalleled. I came to see how car time made space for me to bring forward one of my great gifts and capacities, albeit one I didn't then recognize as such—*listening*. Not a passive or one-way listening, that way of asking for and receiving someone else's one-directional offering. There is a special kind of listening that can only happen over time, and I have come to think of it as one of the great untapped social change resources available to us, if we cultivate the commitment and the sensibilities to utilize it. It is both a listening *to* another and a listening *with* another. Listening *with* implies a common standpoint and/or a common vision or purpose calling you forward. With ongoing presence and engagement, this kind of listening can be generative and creative—*co*-creative.

In those long car rides with John, I was cultivating listening as a generative practice. Generative listening requires actively holding a space of expectation, trust, and appreciation, and inviting depth or creativity, often in the form of a question that sparks reflection. It requires welcoming what wants to grow, and it is supported by an intentional reflecting back, an appreciative mirroring, that can magnify strengths and help a speaker to see their own gifts and skills more clearly and therefore to inhabit them more fully. Our car time allowed me to exercise this kind of listening in the design and practice of peacebuilding programming, and it allowed me to observe how this listening practice supports a unique kind of creativity and practice. John was embodying very similar capacities in his work with the Fambul Tok staff and community leadership.

Feminist theologian Nelle Morton speaks of "hearing others to speech," describing a kind of hearing that is "engaged in by the whole body that evokes speech—a new speech—a new creation." Requiring more than just a listening ear, hearing to speech points to a relational approach to transformation, engaged over time. It is engaged not only with what a person might be saying at the moment but also with a broader knowledge of and commitment to who they are and how they want to go forward in the world. Morton writes:

> We empower one another by hearing the other to speech. We empower the disinherited, the outsider, as we are able to hear them name in their own way their own oppression and suffering. . . . Hearing in this sense can break through political and social structures and image a new system. A great ear at the heart of the universe—at the heart of our common life—hearing human beings to speech—to our own speech.[6]

Though literal hearing takes place within an individual body, I think Morton's idea is also metaphoric for the social body. So what does hearing to speech look like within the social body? Morton's

---

6   Nelle Morton, *The Journey Is Home* (Boston: Beacon Press, 1985), 128.

writing opens us to that imaginative space. By locating this hearing as a divine capacity, an embodiment of the divine ear, she situates this most intimate, relational act explicitly in its full transformational potential. And by asking us to "image a new system," she is signaling a process that is both internal and external, individual and collective. *Imaging a new system* is in many ways exactly what we were doing in that car, in an embodied, mile-by-potholed-mile way. Surprisingly, it felt like simply being human together. And maybe that's the point.

Chapter 11

MAGNIFYING GOODNESS

I laugh loudly.

I didn't even realize that until one of the last gatherings of our two-year Moral Imagination program, a weeklong session in Ethiopia. I arrived late, joining the group on the second day. We exchanged joyful greetings and were just settling back into the meeting when someone wisecracked, and I laughed. Apparently loudly. John Paul smiled and said, almost under his breath, "Ah, there's that Libby laugh. We missed that." I smiled, slightly self-conscious but touched by the appreciative sentiment. Now that I was aware of it, I was surprised to discover that my laugh was in fact kind of singular, not just for its volume but for its spontaneity and genuine joyfulness. JP's passing comment gave me a new ability to see and feel that one of the qualities I brought to the group was my embodied joy. His words served as a mirror, reflecting back to me something about who and how I was in the world—one of the resources I brought to my work.

If one offhanded reflection can yield so much insight, what might be possible if we take on appreciative mirroring with more intentionality? In Western cultures that constantly push self-improvement, it is easy to ignore, miss, or undervalue the good that's already there, in others and ourselves. In helping professions, we are conditioned to focus on others' needs, which compounds our blindness to both our own needs and our own strengths. Because it is also easier to see *what* we do than *how* we do it, it is easy to miss or minimize some of our greatest strengths. Sometimes we need each other in order to see ourselves more clearly.

Being an appreciative mirror for positive qualities in others is a powerful way to mobilize and magnify their expression, supporting more generous and generative modes of self-seeing and stronger self-expression. What we appreciate, appreciates. There is great substance and power in things like joy, or wonder, or compassion, or imagination—ways of being that aren't outwardly visible. Yet lived out and magnified, they can transform—a room, a group, a family, a community . . . a country.

Living the story

Though mirroring is individual and relational work, it can also be made manifest in programming. One way Catalyst for Peace has done this is through storytelling. Storytelling is typically envisioned as something that happens separate from or *about* the work, but we have woven storytelling and program practice together in innovative ways. In doing so, we conceptualized our storytelling *as* peacebuilding, instead of merely *about* peacebuilding.

From the beginning, Fambul Tok unfolded on two parallel tracks: the ongoing, emerging program on the ground that John led and the storytelling about that work, centered around a documentary film, which I led. Typically, these two tracks don't go together. Journalism separates the telling of a story from the doing of the work, a division often considered crucial for journalistic integrity. And in the delicate work of transformation, whether individual or communal, outside observation and documentation, especially in film, can easily disrupt or even destroy the sacred space that holds the work.

Even in Fambul Tok's early days, we imagined these parallel tracks in mutually healthy relationship, and we each had distinct roles. For John to allow a crew to film the process and program as it unfolded, he needed a guarantee that the program, and ultimately the community and the people's needs, came first. Always. And if he ever felt like the film crew's presence would in any way jeopardize or interfere with those needs, he needed the authority to call it off.

Because of my unique role, I was able to make that promise and hold that space. I stood between the film and the program, believing fully in the vision and potential and integrity of both. I could hold them apart, when needed, for the integrity of each and weave them together when the weaving made something stronger.

John, Sara (the film director), and I, along with our immediate teams, were dialogical in everything we did, and our conversations became real-time processing channels for the rapidly unfolding events on the ground. The clarity that emerged from those conversations filtered back iteratively into our written materials and the unfolding program. It became very difficult to say who was the "author" of much of our early documentation; we all contributed needfully to its articulation. Given our practice of emergent design, it was as if the work itself was a narrative formation process—like we were literally writing our story into being, in word and image and deed at the same time.

When John introduced the film crew to the communities, he emphasized that we wanted to film because the world had much to learn from them and from the *fambul tok* process. But we never took communities' acceptance of our filming plans for granted. In fact, at the first ceremony in Bomaru, when it seemed like the presence of white people might distract from the integrity of the *fambul tok* process, John asked the film crew, and me, to stay away. We agreed without hesitation. As the evening progressed, we were invited back by Bomaru's leaders—and able to film.

Initially, I had conceived of the film as serving international audiences, but as Fambul Tok spread across Sierra Leone, we saw storytelling feeding back into and strengthening the work on the ground in unanticipated ways. Like the Manowan elder who noted the power of being asked what *they* wanted to do and how, we witnessed communities' pride in having their cultural strengths valued and amplified as something positive to share with and teach the world. We saw that our seeing was a source of inspiration and agency to them, as well as an invitation to recognize that potential themselves and to step into it more fully. Having others recognize that you have a gift to give the world can motivate and inspire you to bring your best to the task at hand.

Catalyst's commitment to invest heavily in filming without knowing exactly what would emerge honored the value of the work and of the people leading it. It grounded the work in affirmation and faithful expectancy, and it nourished the work and invited people's best. Our storytelling commitment held the space of the work's global significance from the beginning and embodied the core assumption that how you see something impacts what you see. Looking for something creates space for it to come forward and be seen, recognized, and valued. A storytelling lens that looks for and recognizes the resources that are already there in a culture and community is powerful, in a parallel way to the program lens that does the same thing. Stories crafted using this lens become positive mirrors back to the culture and communities themselves, helping people see things about themselves that they might not have otherwise recognized or valued.

Our whole program vision and design was, in reality, narrative formation. We were living into being the story we wanted to be telling—through the work we did, the *way* we did it, and the way we shared about it. The way we embedded storytelling within our program and process gave us concrete tools for that weaving from the start.

Sara's participation in our early planning meetings, beyond helping coordinate the filming, supported program development in critical ways. With her storyteller's sensibility and her own extensive global experience, she was able to mirror back to the program leaders the narratives she saw emerging, helping us to name and therefore to understand the work in newly strengthened ways. She also helped contextualize the work within national and international dynamics and trends, which in turn supported our ability to speak about its global significance to the communities and the broader public, including through Sierra Leonean media. Sara was our embedded "outside eye." Her involvement happened almost by accident in the beginning, but if I did it all over again, I would want a communications professional involved in the program planning from the start.

The physical pieces we produced for global audiences also fed back into the program directly. I have a vivid memory of arriving in Kailahun Town, the first annual report in hand. The report was a small, vibrantly colored book, full of Sara's evocative photos of Fambul Tok in action, with text I wrote explaining the work and quotes from various community members conveying their experiences of the program. The report was primarily intended to share the power of the stories emerging from Fambul Tok's work and unique approach, in a way that captured the spirit and the substance of the work—to speak from the heart of the work to the hearts of people around the world. I remember seeing Isata Ndoleh, a local elder and Mommy Queen, seated at the lone café in the town center. I walked over to say hello and asked excitedly if she'd seen the report. "Oh, you mean our book! You have a copy of our book!" she exclaimed, reaching forward to grab it. She flipped through the pages, recounting stories and pointing out the photos, quotes, and names of people she knew, joyous at finding her own. It was the best compliment I could imagine—that she felt like this publication, written and designed by outsiders, was *theirs*.

The report became the basis of Fambul Tok's training in new communities, a backbone of the unfolding work itself. Its vivid visuals made the report accessible, uniquely suited for training in a culture that is so image-rich and where so many cannot read and write. While this wasn't the purpose we had designed the report for, it became clear that this was one of the unintended positive consequences of our approach to storytelling.

Weaving storytelling into our work became a channel for supporting and strengthening the *organic* emergence of the work, for growing it in contextually grounded ways—for building it *from the inside out*. We recognized the cyclical amplifying power of human-centered story, like an echo that multiplies and builds, connected to human-centered transformational programming, and we built a home for the two to play together in mutual, ongoing relationship.

Good somebodies

The power of this cycle played out perhaps most notably with Mohamed Savage, the notorious commander who went through a reconciliation process with the communities where he had committed countless atrocities. After all he had done and all he had been through, it was the heartfelt, heartbroken words of a sister pleading to her brother that touched and transformed him. Not a powerful authority figure. Not a prison cell. But human-to-human connection, conveyed through film, "brought life back to" him, in his words. The intimacy of relational connection invited him to see himself as more than the monster who had committed atrocities during the war. That connection invited him to be simply . . . human.

Three years later, in May of 2012, Mohamed carried that invitation forward to others, amplifying it in new ways by using his own story to invite other ex-combatants to transform their own lives. It was a national election year in Sierra Leone, and Fambul Tok was chairing a UN-funded collaboration of more than 70 civil society organizations working to prevent election violence. The campaign's first official activities were starting in Waterloo, the informal community just outside Freetown, where more than nine thousand ex-combatants lived, and Mohamed Savage was taking the lead as Fambul Tok's representative there.

The campaign kickoff coincided with one of my regular visits, and on this trip, I had brought a Krio-dubbed version of our feature film, shortened for broadcast and updated with footage following Mohamed's return to Kono and his reconciliation ceremony. John recognized the kickoff in Waterloo as an opportunity to screen the film for ex-combatants. Mohamed suggested we hold a workshop to accompany the screening, so we set aside a full day and invited 30 to 40 influential members of the community.

Mohamed was very keen to have his story shared with other ex-combatants, but John and I had no idea how the film and Fambul Tok in general would be received by the group. Frankly, we anticipated resistance to engaging with the ideas of nonviolence and reconciliation in any depth. We couldn't have been more wrong.

On the day of the event, eager ex-combatants kept appearing until there were more than 60. John and Mohamed co-facilitated. John opened the program by asking everyone to introduce themselves and say one thing they would like to learn that day. The responses set the tone, illuminating the heartfelt motivations drawing people to the meeting:

"I want to be a good somebody in the community."

"I want to get the skills to live in peace with our communities."

"I want to help prepare [ex-combatants] to be changed people."

"I want to become united so we can create a better image."

"I sell drugs. I do it because I haven't had another way to be constructively engaged. I am looking to learn things that will help me be constructive so I won't sell drugs anymore."

"During the past elections, no one engaged ex-combatants. Doing it this time sends the signal that we can be peaceful, nonviolent."

These responses and others like it dispelled any doubts we had about whether this group was interested in embracing nonviolence.

We settled in to watch the Krio version of the film. It was an almost out-of-body experience to sit next to Mohamed Savage, watching the other ex-combatants watch his story unfold. Many of them sobbed during the screening. Several were so moved, they had to get up and leave. But the most extraordinary moment was after the screening, when Mohamed stood up to speak. With singular focus and eloquence, he urged his fellow ex-combatants to change their ways. He urged them to acknowledge the wrong they had done during the war and to apologize and reconcile, not only with the communities they had wronged but also with themselves. He urged them to commit to nonviolence, and he talked about the resistance they would face in that process. That powerful forces would try to lure them back to their old ways. That their friends and acquaintances wouldn't immediately accept that they had changed, and that they would have to be patient and persistent in going forward anyway. He said that when he went back to apologize, he had done so not only for himself and his community but also for *them*, the ex-combatants gathered in front of him—to be an example to them and to help them do the same thing.

John asked the group what they thought about the film and Savage's story and how many of them might want to follow Savage's example and reconcile with the communities they had hurt. Every single person in the room raised their hand. Every. Single. Person.

In smaller group conversations, several said that they saw the war as "senseless and wicked" and that they felt fierce regret while watching the film. Many said it was the first time they realized the kind of pain they had caused others in the war. They also acknowledged that, in their own reconciliation processes, the first task would be to prepare "inwardly." They knew it would take work for them to be emotionally ready to apologize—to face the truth of their actions fully and honestly and to be ready to face others' responses, whatever they may be. They wanted to embrace this work as their next task.

There was a clear recognition that many had fought in the war because they had been manipulated by politicians, or by others in senior positions. They saw that dynamic as ongoing, given that they were almost all still being recruited to foment violence for political purposes. Savage described the intense pressures he continued to face along these lines, accompanied by huge financial incentives. He had been able to resist these pressures with the support of the community and relationships he had forged with Fambul Tok. Now, the group of ex-combatants was pledging to become that kind of support network for each other. Both during and after the war, they had affirmed their loyalty to their recruiters by repeating the slogan "A dae wit you" (I am with you). The expression was a survival mechanism, one that secured a measure of safety for anyone who spoke it. But now, they saw the sense of belonging it offered as illusory, demeaning, and manipulative. They rejected the slogan and instead declared a strong and countervailing commitment to organize now for good, for self-improvement, and for community welfare.

Moving forward, they decided that they no longer wanted their identities to be defined by their actions in the war. Instead of being known as "ex-combatants," they wanted to define their group identity for themselves, with a term that expressed what they wanted to be in their communities going forward. After lively discussion, they adopted the term "Peace Parents." Names matter: they were choosing not only a new identity, one in which they had full agency, but also a conceptual home for the opportunity they wanted to claim. They knew that the work of bringing peace in their communities going forward wasn't one-off and wouldn't bring instant results. But rather, like parenting, it would take long-term commitment and careful tending and nurturing.

Together, they decided on the criteria for Peace Parents: committing to nonviolence, in action and in communication; reconciling with your people; and being productively engaged in your communities and in providing community service.

John summed up the day by saying how much he had learned. He reflected back that he now saw that ex-combatants were not bad people but simply people who needed another opportunity. Mohamed's story was helping the newly christened Peace Parents see, and take, that opportunity. His example and his words were creating a powerful, generous, generative invitation to transformation, similar to the one he had been given—if they were willing to walk toward it. Which they clearly were.

Braiding it all together

At that screening and the workshop that followed, John, too, was an outsider. He modeled the primary role we have crafted for someone providing outside accompaniment—*learning*. Not an abstract, intellectual learning but learning-in-practice. Grounded, contextualized, active, expectant. John learned a lot that day because he entered the session *willing* to learn, and his willingness to learn was part of the container for the full learning and transformation that happened that day. It wasn't a passive willingness—a mere "I'll go in and see if I hear something I didn't already know." It was a proactive willingness to make the space for, invite, and engage with people as people, in their full humanness. To invite all, including himself, to learning and new action, in a way that was rooted in expectancy and trust in the power of people's fundamental goodness, even if that goodness might have been overtaken or obscured. There was no blindness, willful or otherwise, to the real harm done in the past or to the incentives to repeat harm in the present. But there was a willingness to hold the space for people to be present as their whole selves, the good and the bad, and not simply as a stereotype or label, especially a label rooted in past actions and the complexities of Sierra Leone's civil war. As one man noted at the beginning of the day, simply being engaged as potential allies in preventing election violence gave them an invitation and permission to be peaceful.

All of this illuminates a broader dynamic we have found in our work: that when an outsider goes in as a learner, it can call forward all the good that people, communities, or cultures have to teach. When we commit to learning alongside the people we are working to help, we are actively creating space for them to learn and grow as well, and for the work we do with them to be mutually enriching. If what we appreciate, appreciates, then what we are willing to learn comes forward to teach us.

That has implications for both programming and storytelling, both of which can be practiced through the lens of an invitation to be taught. Especially in settings where people are used to being ignored or dismissed, bringing this approach opens a generous and generative space that can by itself open new identity formation for those whose stories are being documented.

In the workshop that birthed Peace Parents that day, we witnessed the primal desire people have to be "good somebodies," to be positive forces contributing good to their communities. It was a theme we had encountered in all of the bonfire ceremonies I witnessed, where people who had committed atrocities were often the most eager to testify. Many described it as a desire to once again be, and be seen as, someone who makes positive contributions to their community. Similar to this is the other primal desire I witnessed, especially through the Peace Mothers' work—a desire to care for others and ensure the family and community have what they need to grow and thrive. These desires represent precisely the untapped power that Fambul Tok's community-mobilizing process animated, and which the story-sharing cycles embedded throughout every level of the program helped magnify and build upon.

Recognizing the power of those desires is how we built the home for our work. At the heart of that home was our kind of extravagant hospitality, a hospitality centered in inviting people into expression and action, in community, and in sharing their stories with those whom they might help and inspire. We built a home for the *how* as much as the *what*. We built a home for the not-knowing, made possible by trusting that the answers are there. We built a home for reflection, for listening and learning together, whether in the car, over Skype, or in a beautiful retreat center. We cultivated hearing people and communities to speech by committing to emergence in program design. We embedded a long-term, multifaceted vision of storytelling throughout our work as a primary tool to support its growth and magnify all the good we saw happening. And we centered and supported our own learning at every step.

Chapter 12

A HOME OF MY OWN

Losing myself, birthing a Wisdom Circle

By the fall of 2013, Fambul Tok, both the organization and the movement, was a major presence in Sierra Leone and a major inspiration around the world. Over six years, what began as a pilot program in a handful of communities had taken root in more than 2,500 villages across six districts. Rural women who had never before had a voice in the public arena were being seen as leaders and were driving small-scale development that benefited the entire community. As communities healed from the wounds of war, they were working together in new and powerful ways, building things like schools and health centers and solving new conflicts themselves.

In addition to having supported the work on the ground with funding totaling more than $5 million by that point, Catalyst had produced and distributed a feature film to great global acclaim, an accompanying book, and an array of educational and training material. I'd made nearly twenty trips to Sierra Leone to support and learn from every facet of the work, and I had traveled across the US to share its story. There was huge and growing global interest in the approach. For six years, I had invested not just money but the fullness of who I was and who I was growing into. Fambul Tok's success was astounding, and the further potential felt limitless.

In 2009, John and I had incorporated Fambul Tok as an international organization to support similar work around the world. We had adopted a unique hybrid structure to support the global expansion we envisioned, with corporate headquarters in the US at the Catalyst for Peace offices and program headquarters in Sierra Leone. Fambul Tok International effectively subsumed Catalyst for Peace, or CFP, into its new global platform. I felt total synchronicity between my individual and organizational vision and both the ongoing work and the global expansion we planned to grow into, so I felt comfortable with the change.

It quickly became clear, however, that it wasn't the right time for that international growth. Pulled by a sense of the world's need for this way of working, we had felt pressure to grow faster than we were able to, and it stretched us all past what we were able to sustain. We realized that sustainable success in Sierra Leone needed more robust focus and a longer-term commitment, and we didn't want to get distracted by the lure of growth, which is what it felt like was happening.

It also became clear that this hybrid national/international organization wasn't the right structure to support the work or our partnership. The new division of labor meant that I had more direct fiscal responsibilities for the programming in Sierra Leone than I had had as a grantor, and also that John ultimately reported to me. Even with our deep mutual respect and our commitment to working as a partnership (and not as a reporting relationship), the structural demands of the new organization were impossible to get past. It was simply not workable. In fact, it was only *because* of the strength of our partnership, and the depth with which we inhabited the same core ideas and vision, that our ability to work together survived that experiment. After two years, Fambul Tok International was dissolved. We closed down the US-based corporate headquarters and squarely reestablished Fambul Tok as a Sierra Leonean organization, and CFP began to regroup. The hybrid international organizational structure had failed, and its failure was challenging and painful.

Still, we had succeeded in some things and wanted those to last. We had a working collaboration linking local to national to international actors, all sharing common vision, common commitment, and ongoing attention to mutuality of relationship. We made space for creativity, balanced with the organizational discipline needed to support community-centered practice at national scale. We created lively learning-in-practice spaces capable of holding even the most difficult conversations.

I was grateful that John and I remained committed to working together, but disentangling our institutions did not reground me individually or Catalyst for Peace organizationally. I was exhausted, and I was unsure about how to take Catalyst forward. I mourned the loss of Fambul Tok International and what it represented. I also knew there was a next iteration of core purpose yet to unfold, for me and for CFP, and I had neither the clarity of vision nor the energy to discern it. Having poured my whole heart and soul and energy and resources into Fambul Tok in its various expressions, I had poured myself right out. I had nothing left.

For years, I had positioned myself as an invisible support, working behind the scenes. Inviting others forward requires stepping back yourself, and I believed, and still do, that this was necessary and right for the work to succeed, especially given the legacy of colonialism we were working against. I also knew that my own deeper purpose was helping to grow this *way* of working in the world. I realized I had stepped too far back, in the process losing not just my organizational purpose but myself, as a person and as a leader. I had lost my capacity to see, name, and claim my *own* desires and needs; I had become invisible, and so had CFP. By 2013, I had run up against the limits of my capacity to function that way any longer. I needed help reclaiming what was mine to do—which meant it was time to demolish my strong internal barriers to *receiving* the same kind of support I so freely and easily offered to others.

In September of 2013, I gathered a trusted cohort of friends and colleagues for a week on the peaceful shores of Long Lake, Maine, to support me in my leadership, in my growth as a person, and in discerning the way forward for CFP. That group included Amy Potter Czajkowski, a longtime colleague and friend who had been involved with Fambul Tok from the very first day John and I met; Bryan Martin, the president of the KonTerra Group, who had been providing strategic support for Fambul Tok and Catalyst for Peace since our first Vermont retreat; and Charles Gibbs, long a cherished friend and wise colleague, who had just retired that summer after 17 years as the founding executive director of URI. We were also joined by Heather Woodman, a beautiful soul who had provided logistics for many of our past retreats, and who had that rare combination of capacity to bring thoughtful, detailed order and beauty to a space while also sharing penetrating spiritual perspectives in a way that elevated the conversation to the next level. And, of course, John.

While it had become a regular expectation for me to insist the Fambul Tok leadership team take time away from the frontlines of the work in Sierra Leone to reflect and refuel for their own renewed leadership, it was unprecedented for me to ask John to do that for *me*. At a facilitated meeting we'd had a few months before, to help rebuild our working relationship after the dissolution of Fambul Tok International, John had made a bold statement: "You will not be helping me if you don't create a space for me to help you." His words floored me. I knew them to be absolutely sincere and to contain a deeper truth I was only beginning to understand. And it was still difficult for me to ask for such a significant commitment from him, when I knew he was so needed in Sierra Leone. But I leaned into the truth and power of his earlier statement and invited him to come.

It was also difficult for me to ask for and receive presence and support from Charles, who was fresh off his retirement. But I was eager for his partnership, especially in creating the strong spiritual grounding that I wanted and needed for the week, and which I couldn't envision or enact alone. We had remained close friends and colleagues since the Moral Imagination project, including undertaking a joint writing project on living into spiritual leadership. I saw my retreat as a continuation of that exploration, this time in practice instead of through words.

In thinking together about the retreat, Charles shared how helpful he found intentional sacred openings, especially for creating a space that invites the right unfolding of the purpose of a gathering. I had no experience with ceremony and ritual, since there wasn't any in the Christian Science church. And although I had worked to imbue my deepest faith and spiritual values into every aspect of the way I worked, I knew there was more to draw from. Charles and I set about designing an opening activity that would create a sacred container for the week, establishing a depth of interaction and inviting the highest and best of everyone there. I trusted his experience and sensibilities and looked forward to trying something new.

I also worried that a sacred opening might seem inappropriate to Bryan. I had a core commitment to respecting others' boundaries, especially around the spiritual, and I worried that he might experience my introduction of spiritual activity into a "professional" space as an unwelcome crossing of the line between "secular" and "religious." But he welcomed the activity, and I realized my anxieties were actually an indication of my own learning edges.

Charles and I collaborated to create a sacred opening as a whole-body way to open up what I most yearned for and needed in the next phase of my work in the world. Ahead of the retreat, we invited everyone to take time to reflect on their understanding of their own unique purpose and to find an object that symbolized that, or something that inspired them in pursuit of it. Everyone brought their objects to Maine, and to open our time together, we shared our stories. As we began, I set a large wooden bowl in the center of our circle to hold what we had brought. One by one, people put their objects into the bowl and described what they represented. Heather added a beautiful seashell, symbolizing the expansive ocean vistas that signified the spiritual views she opened to for inspiration, and a handful of sand, representing the way she relished even the smallest acts of grace and beauty for how they could settle into and fill any crack, crevice, or open space. Bryan added the racing bib he had worn in a bike race commemorating a friend who had recently died, a friend whose wholehearted joy and generous community activism were a huge inspiration to him. The rest of the offerings were equally rich and equally varied.

I went last. When it was my turn, I sat in the center and held the bowl in my lap—noting that, in reality, I had gone first. The bowl itself represented my core purpose: creating spaces that called forth people's highest purpose and brought them into mutually fruitful relationship with others, in ways that helped make something better for all that no one could have done on their own. I also brought some fun Christmas ornaments and added them to the bowl one by one—a mini loaf of French bread, to represent the ways I fed and nourished the purposeful work; a watering can, to indicate adding inspiration; a spade, to indicate the work of pulling the weeds that might otherwise choke new growth. It was a visual, visceral embodiment of my often invisible work as a "bowl-holder."

But I also noted that I had been so focused on holding and tending the bowl, with others in the middle, that I never had the chance to be in the bowl myself. I knew that I needed to have time and space where I could be "in the middle," where I could experience not just holding but *being held*, in order for me and the work I wanted to lead to go forward and grow. That was my goal for this retreat—to experience a space where I could also be held.

Charles invited me to put down the bowl and stand up, and he invited everyone else to stand in a close circle around me, to create a felt experience of being *in the middle*. I burst into tears, immediately aware of a new sense of the possibility—and, unexpectedly, my worthiness—to be held in this way. After a moment in the middle, I also became uncomfortable, squirming to step back to the edges of the circle and help hold the space for the work of the week and beyond. Ultimately, of course, both are and would be needed. But I had at least declared my yearning publicly—I had taken the first steps on the journey of living into its realization. I was learning, in practice and in community, just how much that required: the self-awareness to recognize I needed it, the confidence to ask for it, the faith to trust that it could be there, and the humility to actually receive it.

One of my bowl-holding activities has always been reflecting back to others the good I see them expressing, in ways that help them recognize and celebrate that good more fully themselves. Before the retreat, Amy had interviewed people who had worked with me in the past, asking them to reflect on what they experienced as the unique dimensions of my leadership. Those of us gathered in Maine did the same with each other, and then we spent the rest of our first day together sharing the results of those interviews.

After listening to just the first one, I was weak in the knees. By the end of the day, I melted into the armchair and literally couldn't move. The feedback from the interviews offered more good than I could absorb. I felt like I had been sprayed with a fire hose, my limbs limp as wet noodles. I couldn't even breathe fully; I could expel, but I couldn't take enough in. It was physically painful to receive that much good. I had experienced only one afternoon of being "in the middle," and I felt I had completely dissolved and disappeared, like a caterpillar in a chrysalis.

The next morning, I *literally* disappeared from the group. The task on the agenda was to categorize ideas and distill themes from the previous day, and I simply had nothing in me. I told Amy, Charles, and Bryan that I felt like I'd had my chest ripped open, and my raw, beating heart lay there, exposed. They let me know that this was OK. It was safe to be raw and open and exposed. Amy invited me to trust what my body was telling me: if I had no energy to give to the next activity, that meant I didn't need to be there, and I was welcome to do whatever else I needed to do, wherever I needed to do it.

So I sat in a rocking chair overlooking the smooth, sparkling lake. I closed my eyes and just rocked, for a longggg time. Later, I found a sunny spot to lie on the ground and rest, listen to music, and just . . . be. I let the others hold the work I had poured my heart and soul into for the last ten years. Hold my heart. Hold *me*.

I felt ready to rejoin the group in the afternoon, although I was unsure if I could do anything more than be present. But as I listened to them describe the morning's work, I was immediately enlivened. The team had so clearly treated the ideas respectfully, appreciatively, and creatively, identifying themes and seeing things I had not recognized myself. It was as if they were holding up a beautiful appreciative mirror that simultaneously made *me* more visible and revealed that the substance of the work was so much bigger than only me.

In one day, I had gone from feeling alone to melting into what felt like nothingness to tenderly sensing and seeing that I was whole, even in my in-process-ness—and that I was also part of a larger whole. The week flowed freely from there, and we were able to plan next directions for Catalyst in ways that sprang fully and meaningfully from *my* own purpose.

The core of this group met regularly over the next two years in what I came to call my Wisdom Circle. Besides tending to soul and role for me as a person and as a leader, the Wisdom Circle was a space of ongoing collective discernment for Catalyst for Peace. It helped me learn-in-practice how to widen the channel for a free, nourishing flow between and among the elements of our work, and it became a channel for individual and organizational wisdom to become operational. Although it took another year and a half for me to make it to the other side of what I describe as my "dark night of the soul," throughout that time the Wisdom Circle was like a womb for the next unfolding of my purpose in the world—a bowl that I could help hold *and* that could hold me. It strengthened CFP's core and supported its emergence into the world in its next iteration. And although it often puzzled me just how, it was clearly a strengthening and soul-nourishing space for all who participated in it.

The week in Maine was singular, but our time together illuminated common themes that called us all and would shape our work together going forward. Amy's reflections about the week illustrate that dual dynamic:

During our time last week, you were able to pull together realms and ways of being that don't usually share the same space. It was an astounding mix of being a space for personal growth and organizational planning, and the purposes flowed back and forth in a natural and uninterrupted rhythm. It was a space for Libby Hoffman to break through personal (and societal) barriers of silence AND identify an organizational agenda for CFP. Everyone there was in service to both. We were friends and professional colleagues, [supporting] both personal and professional development. I was so impressed with your commitment to face even the hardest feelings in order to break through.

From my perspective, the process you were going through paralleled how the role of accompaniment has been stymied and silenced. It hasn't been OK to be human in professional endeavors. And when I have seen people become vulnerable, it's often in a navel-gazing way rather than in letting go for the service of bigger goals and serving others. I saw your willingness to face the challenging inner voice (borrowed from the world) as a way to be of better and greater service to others, and part of that is unleashing your voice about the things that are important to you and that you see clearly. Although we were there for you, you took a lot of responsibility for your own breakthroughs.

At the end of the week, Charles reflected on what a blessing it was for him to have been there. "Like being part of a perfect game in baseball," he wrote, "you can't plan it, anticipate it or force it. No one can accomplish this alone and only very rarely do people accomplish it together—a sustained moment of great effort when individuals' strengths come to the fore and egos dissolve in pursuit of a shared and transcendent purpose." His words illuminated the balance of individual and communal, deep faith and hard work, the singularly personal and the expansively universal that not only characterized our week but also continued to call to us throughout the work of the Wisdom Circle, and even calls to us today. He summed up the week as "a blessing created by courage, vulnerability, clear intention and a small group of extraordinary people with unique experiences and gifts, big hearts, small egos and a profound commitment to be of selfless service."

Those qualities, lived out together, are indeed a roadmap to transformation.

Leaving my father's house

Preparing for the retreat, I had felt a reflexive desire to offer something back to the people coming to support me, perhaps by hosting the event at my dad's home on Clapboard Island, off the coast of Maine. I thought the stunning beauty and the luxurious yet comfortable graciousness of the space might entice people to come, or reward them once they were there. Buried in those thoughts was a fear that my work and I weren't worthy of the support in and of themselves, or that supporting me wouldn't also be rewarding for the people I was inviting. I was afraid that the giving would be one-way, and I was still unready myself to receive from others. I also recognized a subtle worry that maybe I didn't have enough of substance to offer on my own, not just for this retreat but more generally for the work we were called to do next—that I might have to rely instead on my dad's wealth and connections to expand my work more fully into the world.

The other retreat venue I had in mind was a summer camp on Long Lake, a place interwoven in many ways with my family's story. My husband, Seth, was on the board, and all our children had been campers and counselors there. I decided the camp was a perfect place for our retreat, and yet Clapboard Island kept poking my thought.

When I mentioned this nagging thought to Bryan, he noted that an important preparation for moving into a new space is intentionally leaving behind the old. "What do you want to leave behind—to bless and release—from your old house?" Bryan asked. He meant something more than my literal physical space; he was inviting me to consider assumptions, values, and practices that might have been helpful at one point but now no longer served me or the work that I had before me. He suggested I give time and thought to a process of "leaving my father's house" as part of my preparation for moving into and inhabiting the new.

The phrase had both a literal and symbolic meaning for me. I was very conscious of everything positive and valuable that I had received from my parents, and I had strong feelings of loyalty and responsibility to my father, especially since my mother's passing. His labor and accomplishments created the financial resources I was using for Catalyst for Peace, and I had worked hard at keeping my dad informed of and connected with everything I did through CFP. He had come from humble beginnings himself, the youngest of seven children of immigrant parents, and his father had run a poultry store on the South Side of Chicago. The "self-made" nature of his wealth heightened my already keen sense of obligation to keeping him connected with how I was, in turn, giving forward the wealth he had created. While my dad loved and respected me, he seemed fundamentally unable to grasp the value of what I was doing and how I was doing it, though he appreciated it because it was important to me. He had a hard time understanding why anyone would *want* to travel to "developing countries," much less center long-term work and deep relationships there. The concept of anchoring that work in learning from and with the people in these regions, and helping the world do so as well—that was not even on his radar. My work simply didn't fit his understanding of politics and how it was supposed to work—or, for that matter, how money or spiritual practice should work either.

All of that was hard for me to accept. It left me feeling disappointed in my dad and at times discouraged, especially given the efforts I had made to help him understand what I was doing and why. And as much as I didn't want to admit it, I realized I had internalized doubts about my deeper vision and values from being steeped in his worldview my whole life. In Bryan's suggestion to "leave my father's house," I heard an invitation to leave behind that worldview along with both my hope for perfection on my dad's part and my desire for his validation, allowing me to embrace him for the imperfect human being that he is. I heard an invitation to leave behind the cultural assumptions I was steeped in and instead embrace my own unique identity and claim a full, fearless commitment to my vision. It would be an adult iteration of the teenager's individuation process, freeing me to name and claim *my own* home, to decide what is valuable and valued on my own terms.

Charles offered to help me find a process for blessing and releasing what no longer served me. Though I hadn't actually spent much time at my father's Clapboard Island home—by the time he purchased it, I was an adult with two children of my own and a third on the way—we agreed the house would serve well as a symbolic stage. Charles arrived a half-day before the others, and we drove to Handy Boat Dock in Falmouth, where we boarded a little skiff with Rose Lacasse, the island's caretaker extraordinaire. It was a crisp, blue-sky afternoon, warm enough to go without a coat but with enough chill to remind you that fall was coming. Pulling away from the mainland onto the open water invited an exhale, as if the journey itself were saying, "Leave behind all that entangles and limits you," and the sparkle on the water beckoned us ahead. It was impossible not to smile.

When we reached the island, we walked around, and I reflected on and expressed gratitude for all I had received from my family and upbringing and from the world I had grown up in. I was glad to have Charles with me; I felt like I needed help to hold all the good. I came from a loving home and had every opportunity a person could have. My parents had been thoroughly committed to making a contribution to the world, starting in their own communities and family, and they had instilled those values in us. Touring the house and the grounds, the breathtaking beauty enveloped us. My dad and his wife excelled at creating and enhancing beautiful spaces like these, which were similar to the ones I had grown up in—spaces where I had always felt welcomed, held, and inspired. The tour made obvious how my dad had opened up and normalized an extraordinarily large sense of the world for me. Looking down at the dock, I recalled the time I helped tie the lines for President Bush's boat after he drove it up from Kennebunkport. I remembered my conversations on the wide porches that surround the house, where I talked casually with senior government officials and national business leaders. I recalled the ambassadors I had shared breakfast with in my favorite room in the house, the large, open kitchen, with space for cooking and eating and sitting comfortably and talking. It was fun to show Charles the huge dining table where we had brought together grassroots Israeli and Palestinian peacebuilders and senior US policymakers. Equally the volleyball court where fierce family volleyball games were played when Dad and Dawn hosted my husband's (very large) family for their reunion.

After our tour, we unrolled a blanket on an open expanse of

lawn and picnicked overlooking rows upon rows of hydrangeas, their snowball blooms still clinging to stems as they dried in the crisp fall air. The bay shone around us, sprinkled with boats and buoys. I read through a list I had made of things I no longer wanted to carry with me—things I realized I had absorbed from my home or family or the culture around me as I grew up. Although these things had offered me a great deal of privilege, I increasingly felt their shadow side and saw how the assumptions beneath them were weighing me down and holding me back.

I wanted to say "no, thank you" to a matrix of success and power rooted in very narrow definitions of worth: judging someone's worth based on how much political power or social influence they have; or how much money they have, especially if they've made it "themselves"; or what their body looks like, especially believing that skinnier, toned bodies are more worthy of affection. I wanted to leave behind using intellectual arguments or spiritual platitudes as a way of ignoring or bypassing emotions, especially uncomfortable ones. I wanted to leave behind an emphasis on performing instead of connecting; on maintaining perfectionism and control instead of embracing messy creativity, receptivity, and play. I wanted to leave behind faith in some person or entity outside of me that could or would make everything right and safe. I wanted to leave behind any shred of belief that money was the source of my confidence or the substance of my contribution to the world.

The list certainly wasn't comprehensive, but it represented some of the things uppermost in my thought at the time. After talking it through with Charles, I found a patch of dirt, dug a hole, and buried the paper, consigning it to decay and then to fertilize whatever new growth might be ready to spring later from the soil. We boated back to the mainland, and I felt buoyed, both by the gratitude I had felt and named and by having consciously chosen to leave certain baggage behind—although the real leaving is ongoing, everyday work, and it requires ongoing tending and attention.

In the rush and intensity of the retreat that followed, the island visit faded from my thoughts. But the seed of its significance was planted deeply, perhaps like my buried list. The process of leaving behind had been like mental housecleaning, a clearing out to make room to receive the gifts ready to be offered at the retreat.

The physical and spiritual exhaustion I had felt in the lead-up to the retreat had come from a different kind of emptying process, a pouring out of everything I thought I had to give, until I reached a point where I *had* to reach out for help in order to move forward. In receiving from others, I connected to a source much bigger than my own personal reserves, and with it came a humbling lesson about how many more resources there are to draw upon than I might ever realize. I wrote in my journal about an image that had come to me: "It's like I'm this little pitcher of water, and John helped create a space for me to pour my water—share my gifts. We kept growing that space, making it bigger and bigger. I poured the water all out— and discovered there was no bottom. I'm not actually a *container* for that water, but simply a conduit. If I think I'm the source or the holder of it—that's limiting. But it's only in pouring it all out that you discover the unlimited nature of it."

The retreat was a time of great learning, especially about the reciprocity of giving and receiving. Ultimately, we are only able to give—of our gifts, affections, expertise—to the degree we are willing to receive the same from others. And we are only able to receive from others and the world to the degree we are willing, in turn, to leave behind and release the practices, beliefs, and assumptions that no longer serve us.

I've come to see that list I buried as more than a list of discrete things. The items on that list are exemplars of a broken *system*, a system I never really felt at home in. Often, "systems" show up simply as our own thoughts, as internalized beliefs and assumptions that we don't think to question—the kind of beliefs and assumptions I was, and am, working to leave behind. On Clapboard Island and during the Long Lake retreat, I was renouncing a system that demanded constant productivity from me in a way that depleted me and sanctioned the depletion of others; that said waiting and listening are not "productive"; that measured value primarily by outward productivity. I was leaving a system that didn't see, allow for, make space for, or fully support learning, especially learning-in-process. And especially for leaders. A system that said being an expert means knowing everything already and that being in-process is wrong and bad and unnecessary, a distraction from the "real" work we are here to do. I was leaving a system that supposed we could give to others without being willing to also receive from them. That said needing and asking for anything is weakness. That receiving is weakness. That *wanting* is weakness. That we can't trust our innermost desires. That we can fulfill our highest purpose in the world alone, without giving attention to soul. That we need to stick with what is known and safe.

I came to see that I had a choice about whether to inhabit that system or not. I couldn't be part of a larger whole—a whole bigger than my own ego and capacities, a whole that represented and expressed a *healthy* system—while clinging to a myth of aloneness, self-sufficiency, or separation. I had to acknowledge that my capacity did not come from personal heroism, or from my individual resources and capacities, but that it represented a much deeper and more infinite resource, one I was merely tapping into. I had a conviction that the divine will for wholeness was ultimately impelling and supporting this work, inviting us all to see it and yield to it more fully. If that was true, I realized I had to be willing to do that myself, *for* myself, to understand and demonstrate the full integrity of the idea and to keep the flow open and free.

These core questions now guide me at every juncture: Am I as willing to *receive* as I am to give all that the work requires? Am I as willing to *be transformed myself* as I am to support others' transformation? There is power in the flow, in the back and forth, in the mutuality. The invitation, as the poet David Whyte describes it, is to "put down the weight of your aloneness and ease into / the conversation. . . . / Everything is waiting for you."[7]

The work we've been championing in Sierra Leone is heart-tending work. In the global home we were building for that work, I realized I needed a room of my own. I needed a space where my own heart could also be tenderly, appreciatively held. As I saw and claimed that space, I was able to inhabit the larger home as truly . . . mine.

---

7   David Whyte, "Everything is Waiting for You," in *River Flow: New & Selected Poems* (Langley, WA: Many Rivers Press, 2007), 359.

Part IV

GROWING FROM OUR CORE

Chapter 13

THE RESILIENCE OF RENEWAL

Ebola strikes

When Finda Nyuma died from Ebola in April of 2014, no one in her small community knew exactly what mysterious and merciless disease had taken her life. Finda had unwittingly brought the disease to her village of Kpoundu, in Kailahun District, after caring for a friend in a nearby village. She had been an active and respected elder, and mourners poured in to pay their respects; the disease quickly spread.

Ebola hadn't been seen in Sierra Leone before. Most people had never heard of it, and certainly didn't know how to prevent it. Just a few weeks after Finda Nyuma died, the number of Ebola cases in Sierra Leone jumped to more than 100. Within a month, the country had declared a state of emergency in Kailahun, closing schools and public entertainment places and closing its borders with Guinea and Liberia. Still, the disease spread, and by mid-September, there were more than 1,100 cases nationwide. By December, there were 100 new cases a day across the country. It was exploding just as rapidly in neighboring Guinea and Liberia.

Before the disease finally burned out in the spring of 2016, there were nearly 30,000 cases and more than 11,000 deaths in West Africa. Sierra Leone accounted for nearly half of those cases, and just under 4,000 deaths. It was the most widespread Ebola outbreak in history, causing major loss of life and widespread socioeconomic disruption in the region, and it sparked global concern bordering on panic. In September of 2014, the United Nations Security Council declared the outbreak a "threat to international peace and security," the first time the Council had ever designated a public health crisis as a security threat. Cosponsored by 134 countries, the Council's resolution was also the most broadly supported since 1945. Billions of dollars in aid followed, from dozens of countries, international organizations, and humanitarian agencies around the world.

In Kailahun, the disease tore through ordinary life in unrecognized ways. In the early days of the outbreak, no one realized that the everyday interactions of rural life, especially in caring for the sick or tending the dead, were fueling the spread of the disease. Preparing bodies for burial, for example, required human touch. Meanwhile, neighbors suspected of having Ebola disappeared into treatment centers, where many of them died. With little to no communication between the treatment centers and the families and communities of the sick, many people concluded that the treatment centers *caused* their loved ones' deaths. Neighbors turned against each other, blaming each other rather than the disease for the deaths, in the process causing devastating new community conflicts.

All of this confusion, coupled with anger and no small amount of fear, made communities more resistant to prevention and response protocols recommended by the government and international organizations. Programming and messaging from outsiders were treated with such deep skepticism that they were often suspected of having malicious intent. Rooted in the local population's long history of being ignored, taken advantage of, or imposed upon for someone else's agenda, this distrust, though outwardly invisible, was in many ways the most insurmountable obstacle to stopping the spread of Ebola. And it was something that no amount of money—not even the billions coming into the country—could overcome.

In fact, much of that money was being used in ways that deepened local distrust. For example, the government launched a massive soap distribution campaign to improve basic hygiene, a critical part of Ebola prevention that can be difficult in rural areas with no running water or readily available soap. Distributed along with the official-looking soap were official-sounding messages about the importance of proper handwashing. In many communities, however, people assumed the government was trying to *give* them the disease through the soap in order to gain political advantage by killing off people in their region. It wasn't that distributing soap itself was problematic but that doing so without having first built trust only served to intensify the communities' existing *mis*trust.

Unlike unknown or untrusted outsiders, Fambul Tok's Peace Mothers groups and its Reconciliation Committees had the relationships and connections, built over time, that create trust. Peace Mothers proved to be ideal community educators, coming from and already engaged in the communities themselves. So Fambul

Tok helped educate and mobilize them for Ebola response. Some Peace Mothers groups were even already producing (trusted) soap as part of their microenterprise initiatives; Fambul Tok helped these Peace Mothers scale up their production and worked with others to distribute the soap to their communities, using it as an entry point for community education on disease prevention. The soap, and the messages, were easily received and effective—a vivid demonstration of the unique power and potential of Fambul Tok's combination of local, relationally rooted networks with national organizing capacity.

Fambul Tok's long history of community work also gave the organization insight into how best to communicate general prevention messages. Staff designed image-oriented materials, with pictures of people who looked like local residents, to educate a largely illiterate population about important practices in preventing the spread of Ebola—an approach that stood in unfortunate contrast to the text-heavy materials with unfamiliar images distributed by the government and international nongovernmental organizations (INGOs). Peace Mothers shared these and other forms of public health messaging by activating trusted relationships to spread general preventive messaging—working through relationships that had been (re)forged through Fambul Tok's community reconciliation approach.

The local expertise, energy, and relationships that made Fambul Tok's interventions so successful were largely absent among key actors in the national and international response. Large INGOs received an influx of funding to address the crisis across the region, but they lacked the local networks or infrastructure that would have made that aid more effective. Though they could have worked through local partners who did have those resources, INGOs instead ignored or bypassed local capacity.

Meanwhile, they spent their money in maddeningly irrelevant ways. One Irish NGO received millions to build a coordination app, something far removed from the realities of life in a country where most people don't have or use smartphones. External experts with short-term contracts flooded the country's luxury resorts, removing themselves even further from the realities they did not understand, without appearing to acknowledge that disconnection. The British government headquartered its response team in Sierra Leone's most picturesque getaways, renting out whole beachside resorts for months.

Even efforts intended to solicit "local" input were clumsy. On her October 2014 visit to Sierra Leone, Samantha Power, then the US ambassador to the United Nations, convened a meeting of the major nongovernmental organizations leading Sierra Leone's Ebola response and prevention. No doubt she wanted to ensure that she was hearing local and community voices and perspectives, and yet John was the only Sierra Leonean in the room.

John and I spoke at least weekly, if not more often, during the crisis, and every week he described the same thing: international efforts were disconnected from and ignoring local experience and expertise, especially from the communities themselves.

It was the same dynamic John remembered from the flood of postwar aid: the issues and problems were being defined by outsiders, who also designed and built the solutions; outsiders then came and plopped those "solutions" into the middle of a community to whom they felt, quite often, irrelevant—and with the expectation that Sierra Leoneans would be grateful recipients.

"It's like Sierra Leone is being recolonized by aid," John said in one conversation. "The large international NGOs are spearheading the response, and they have well-oiled machines—but no local structures or credibility in the eyes of the community. It's colonization by compassion."

John thought that ignoring the capacity of local communities to respond meaningfully to this new crisis further disempowered them and, therefore, destabilized wider society. It also left untapped community resources whose plentiful depths we had seen enable great things. "We are not just victims," he said. "We are leaders, and potential leaders. We are agents of change and agents of healing, agents of transformation. That needs to be built on rather than ignored."

John felt there was much more he could do for his country; he just didn't have the channels, given the way the humanitarian aid system was structured, nor did he really have the invitation. His frustration pinpointed the brokenness of that aid system, a system that did not see the community—the place where people live, both geographically and conceptually, in a web of interconnected relationships that are a source of so much of people's identity in Sierra Leone. And yet the community is a living entity, and it is seen and experienced as such by ordinary Sierra Leoneans in a myriad of tangible and intangible ways—ways that Fambul Tok, over the previous seven years, had recognized and strengthened.

John could see so clearly what so many other "experts" could not: Ebola was not just a health emergency requiring medical response; it was also a *community* problem, one that required community action and attention. Truly tackling the Ebola problem meant addressing the community fear and mistrust that were inhibiting effective response. It meant actively mobilizing communities to lead in their own prevention and recovery. This required a reorientation on the part of outside experts and helpers, from seeing the people of Sierra Leone as "victims" to recognizing them as leaders and potential leaders in the response. All of these things were ignored in a narrow focus on treating the disease.

In short, there was a huge gap between the national response and local communities, one that made effective communication and community mobilization virtually impossible. Sierra Leonean civil society organizations had the potential to bridge that gap, if they could organize and collaborate effectively in shared purpose to do so.

This, of course, was work John and his team were uniquely suited to lead, and it was work I was thrilled to support. One example of an early and critical success was a meeting Fambul Tok convened in Kailahun District between leaders from the US Embassy and the district's rural citizens and community-based organizations. The meeting helped Embassy leaders understand how poor communication with families whose loved ones had been taken to Ebola treatment centers fostered mistrust, caused community conflicts, and discouraged people from reporting new suspected cases. The US ambassador helped facilitate new communication protocols for treatment centers so that these issues didn't continue to happen.

Building on that success, Fambul Tok formed a network with other civil society organizations to create stronger links between local communities and national and international actors in a more systematic way; it was called the Bridging Community Network, or BCN. One early BCN district meeting uncovered a need for including women in the burial teams. Without gender-sensitive burial teams, people felt that their dignity was being violated, and they strongly pushed back against the official burial protocols, which were critical in preventing the spread of the virus. With BCN advocacy, the recommendation for including women on all burial teams was adopted.

The BCN held similar consultations in districts across the country. These meetings mobilized and educated local populations, and they made community needs and perspectives clearer to those shaping and implementing policy. It was slow and painstaking work to build the relationships that opened the channels for this kind of constructive and two-way vertical communication, but when it happened, the impact was immediate.

Still, John and I believed there was more we could do, and more Fambul Tok and its model could contribute. Local Fambul Tok structures had been effective in responding to Ebola, confirming our foundational belief that helping communities heal from war would strengthen them to better respond to future crises. We wanted to apply our learning, our philosophy, and our systems thinking to the Ebola response, pushing international actors beyond merely responding to an emergency and toward using aid to build community capacity to lead the recovery. We knew this would, in turn, create *more* community-grounded capacity to respond quickly and effectively to whatever crises these communities might face in the future. We thought of this work as creating social immunity. Needless to say, we wanted to do everything in our power to help our experience and perspective ground the Ebola and post-Ebola response.

"It doesn't have to be that way"

I was continually amazed at John's capacity to sustain his commitment to his work in the Ebola context—difficult in itself, but reinforced by the way the aid system seemed to make it *harder* for leaders like him, with strong community connections and sensibilities. Having been embedded with John in community-centered work for nearly a decade, I could both see and viscerally feel the ways in which the international Ebola response was embodying and reinforcing a notion of division between the people perceived as having the resources and capacity to solve the problems (outsiders), and the (local) people perceived as having only needs. We knew from our experience that this would only further alienate local communities, undermine any trust in outsiders, and further fracture community bonds, diminishing the energy people and communities had for their recovery and development. That, in turn, would only perpetuate dependency on outside aid.

The recolonization John perceived felt like a real threat—something I felt in my body—and mobilizing to prevent it became a core commitment for me and the primary goal of our work and partnership. Alongside a thunderous inner call to prevent that recolonization was a quieter conviction, one I felt gently knocking on the door of my consciousness: "It doesn't have to be that way."

It doesn't have to be that way.

When I could quiet my mind, when I could go deeper than my feelings of urgency and helplessness, I could somehow, from somewhere, hear that message. Ebola response and recovery doesn't have to continue the pattern of leaving local people and communities worse off. It doesn't have to deplete the people trying to give help and support.

It doesn't have to be that way.

It can be done differently.

One voice that spoke that message was the voice of my own embodied experience. We ourselves have done crisis response and recovery differently. Not only can it be done, it *has* been done—in a way that can actually inspire, enliven, restore, and strengthen . . . everyone.

I also heard the message in another way—as a vision, an anticipatory sensing and trust that Sierra Leone didn't have to follow the well-worn grooves of a broken neocolonial system. Sierra Leone, and Fambul Tok, and CFP, and others—we could all act instead from the already-not-yet of a healthy, regenerative system. I sensed that holding this vision and conviction would help open new possibilities, new ways of working that could embody a new, healthy, whole system, one that would help people and communities thrive and step into their full potential.

Although the common aid-community language of "local consultation" and "local ownership" seemed ironic in a system that effectively marginalized both, I also saw such buzzwords as indicating a ripeness for learning how to work differently. The Ebola crisis precipitated a growing recognition that ignoring communities wasn't working, even if there wasn't yet a broad understanding of alternative approaches.

Our next task would be to listen for how we might be called to embody a different, healthier system, and to help make it more visibly real to others—a task that, despite the clarity of the calling, nevertheless felt like moving, slowly and uncertainly, through a thick fog.

Something John said during that time cut through the fog for me. Speaking of the panoply of outsiders whose methods seemed to be making things harder for communities, he said, "They think they can just come and pour resources at the problem, to fix it. They don't even see the community that the problem is happening *in*. That community is like a bowl—and it's cracked. If you pour water into a cracked bowl, it just goes right through. And if you keep pouring, it only makes the cracks bigger."

The metaphor came alive to me. The bowl itself—the container that is the community—was invisible in the way most aid was administered. So *of course* the work of repairing the bowl, of patching its cracks, was equally invisible. And yet that was precisely the work that Fambul Tok had been doing. Fambul Tok and Catalyst for Peace hadn't simply been pouring water—money—in. We had been focused on repairing the cracks in the community container—bringing people together in common purpose, healing relationships, and establishing new communal norms and channels of engagement.

That work enabled communities to hold the water, or aid, that might come from the outside. The metaphor also revealed something more: when the bowl was whole, it seemed to be not just a bowl but a well—tapping into the deep reserves of groundwater right there in the communities themselves. The presence of a healing, whole, healthy community unleashed incredible energy in community members to act on behalf of the communal whole. It was as if people discovered energy and agency they hadn't even known they had, which were only released when and as they worked together on behalf of the whole. We saw example after example of people spontaneously mobilizing to better their communities, whether by building roads and schools or tackling local social issues like teenage pregnancy and domestic violence.

Voicing the work

After a year with my Wisdom Circle, I, too, was working differently. I had, in essence, built my *own* bowl: a community for supporting leadership of this work, a bowl that held me. Inside this bowl, I had been able to see and name the dimensions of accompaniment our team at Catalyst for Peace had embodied over the years of working with Fambul Tok, and I was beginning to see and name the larger framework our work was also embodying. I built a committed writing practice around that, finally making space for giving voice and visibility to the work I had devoted so much of my heart and soul to, not to mention my time and resources. It was still difficult to stand squarely and visibly in *my* presence, *my* experience, and *my* voice in and of that work. But I felt a call, and a growing permission, to do just that.

I also felt a strong and growing desire to openly challenge the larger pattern of international Ebola response and to speak more powerfully and directly from the platform of our work, calling others to see in our lived experience a model for working differently. I had seen that our approach created effective space for addressing pressing, urgent needs and that it did so in a way that unleashed longer-term capacity for change and leadership within communities. I couldn't *not* share this learning, and I couldn't *not* work to leverage our experience with Fambul Tok to try and shift the dominant mode of national and international response. The moment felt ripe for it. International actors were viscerally experiencing the impact of rural populations' lack of trust for outsiders, seeing that frayed social fabric and broken communities made containing Ebola very difficult.

And yet the fear and urgency that the crisis engendered, coupled with the massive amounts of money that came pouring into

Sierra Leone as a result, made reflection and behavioral change difficult. It is hard to think long-term in the middle of an urgent crisis, and it's hard to think in terms of community and relational infrastructure when there is also a pressing need for physical infrastructure, such as treatment facilities and equipment.

Nevertheless, a broader conversation was clearly needed, and I felt we were uniquely placed to spark and lead it. We had a national-scale embodied example of crisis response and recovery that worked from the inside out. The time had come to leverage this experience and engage the national and international aid communities more directly—or, to borrow John's imagery, which is now central to our theory of change, to share with the world how we had learned to repair the community bowl so that it can better hold the resources that pour in, and better draw upon and magnify the community's own resources.

Together, John and I and our organizations began to plan a national dialogue, which we called Catalyzing Healthy Partnerships, between international donors and national civil society. We wrote a policy paper describing the potential we saw in a community-centered Ebola response and announcing a national dialogue that would center on our key questions: What would need to change to create a *healthy system of recovery and development* that sustains both communities and "outsiders" providing support? How could that change happen?

John represented CFP directly as our senior fellow, which opened different channels of access than he was typically accorded as the leader of a local NGO. He met with national and international leadership from multiple sectors, virtually all of whom expressed strong positive interest in the ideas and the dialogue, in the form of a national conference. But John and I quickly realized that a single event wasn't enough. Conversations with national and international stakeholders alone would feel too abstract and disconnected to have a real impact in the long run—this couldn't be a conversation only among outsiders. We also wondered how we could center community voices in an event like that. John made the point that Fambul Tok's bread and butter was engagement at the community level, and that answers to our key questions would and should emerge most clearly in practice, in an embodied way, from within the communities themselves. We committed to building a lived model of *how* to create a system of recovery and development at the community level, and doing so in a way that put the local people in the lead, strengthening the community "container" far into the future. And we committed to creating the channels for those voices to lead the recovery conversation, step by step.

Birthing a People's Planning Process

By spring of 2015, more districts were Ebola-free, or nearly, but the new waves of devastation—physical, psychic, and communal—washing over Sierra Leone had not even begun to be addressed. Fambul Tok began adapting its community healing process to focus on Ebola recovery while positioning communities to lead the planning of what they wanted and needed for their ongoing development.

The work began as a pilot, but John and I held a larger vision for it from the beginning. We wanted this new phase of work not simply to respond to communities' immediate needs as they articulated them but to build a living example of a whole, healthy system working from the inside out—led by communities themselves, supported in healthy and enlivening ways by outside actors. Viewed from this perspective, our pilot wasn't the usual proof of concept: it embodied the concept. The People's Planning Process (PPP), as this work came to be known, didn't try to demonstrate the possibility of working differently. It simply worked differently. From the very beginning, we worked together—funder, international partner, national staff, local leaders, and communities—to live into the system as we believed it could and should be.

John and I envisioned growing this locally centered process nationally as well as speaking into the national context *about* a locally led, community-centered process. We wanted that conversation to happen with local people and communities at the center, leading the discussion. We knew we couldn't really do one without the other. We also knew that, although the context was new, this *way* of working had been at the heart of Fambul Tok and the people who made it what it was all along. "I used to speak on behalf of marginalized communities," John had said years before. "Now I create space for them to speak for themselves." Growing our work to respond to Ebola and catalyze economic development was a natural evolution of that same vision and practice.

The work itself began, once again, in Kailahun District, this time in Kissi Teng Chiefdom, ground zero for Ebola in the country. Like the earlier community reconciliation work, the PPP involved gathering people in widening circles, from village to section and ultimately to chiefdom, and inviting them to consider questions that facilitated their own plans for recovery and development. By the time the pilot was complete, the People's Planning Process would find such support and success that these local-level conversations connected into district governance and ultimately national policy. But first, it all began by gathering villagers.

Four core questions shaped these initial conversations, beginning with attention to Ebola prevention and building from there:

1. What could you do to make sure that Ebola doesn't come into your communities and region again?

2. How would you define your most important peace and development needs?

3. What resources do you have already to begin addressing them?

4. What outside support do you need in order to move forward with your priority needs?

Similar to the community bonfires, the PPP was not designed to be a single event but rather to establish community structures that would carry the work forward, with facilitation support from Fambul Tok only until communities could take the process over themselves. In each section, Community Welfare and Mediation Committees (CWMCs), an evolution of the earlier Reconciliation Committees that still held the inclusive membership values that underpinned them, anchored and drove the process. The committees brought together youth and elders, Muslims and Christians, women and men, those in formal and informal leadership positions. Peace Mothers groups continued as a companion structure, establishing channels for women's broader leadership on behalf of their communities.

Over the course of a few months, Fambul Tok supported each of the five sections of Kissi Teng Chiefdom through creating CWMCs and Peace Mothers groups, and developing their own People's Plan—establishing their own priorities, identifying resources they already had to put toward these priorities, and specifying what help they most needed from outsiders. Each section then designated representatives to meet together, aggregate those plans, and approve a chiefdom-wide People's Plan. Together they also formed an Inclusive Chiefdom Committee, with representation from each CWMC, to oversee the plan's implementation. The Inclusive Chiefdom Committee's role was also to interface with the district-level government entities charged with overseeing development in the district.

Knowing from experience how important it was to anchor the local work in women's leadership, and also how much intentional focus and work it took to do that, in the initial training and communal conversation held at the sectional level, Fambul Tok asked each village to designate two females and one male to represent them—a proportion that our experience had shown effectively guards against the usual absence or silence of women in these meetings. These appointed representatives connected the conversation back to their villages, both sharing ideas and soliciting input. In this way, Fambul Tok's support for local ownership of the PPP also strengthened women's public visibility as leaders in their communities.

Convening people to discuss those four key questions, building out local support structures, inviting collective action to address needs, and identifying and mobilizing human resources already available for the work—doing all of this in a place like Kpoundu, where this book begins, might seem improbable. And yet in Kpoundu and the other villages in Kissi Teng, the community response to the PPP was nothing less than astonishing. The process sparked local interest and energy and catalyzed a commitment to work together on behalf of the community. The CWMCs and Peace Mothers groups took on active development projects for their communities, from soapmaking to small-market initiatives to community farms. With the money they made, they began addressing local needs—paying school fees for children without means, building health posts, building community centers or schools—as they had prioritized them.

The communities were repairing the cracks in their bowls, and now they could tap into rich reserves of "groundwater"—their own energy and resources to work for the common good—and, in the process, re-enliven their communities.

Growing inclusive governance

We believed from the beginning that the community-based PPP should connect to local governance and planning processes so that the people charged with overseeing development in the districts could hear and act on communities' voices and ideas, and so that the process could sustain itself and grow. This connection would be the key to the PPP model taking root in other chiefdoms across the district. We began to realize that connecting the pilot in Kissi Teng Chiefdom with district-level actors in charge of Ebola response and of development was the right next step.

At the same time, we circled back to the idea of a national conference among high-level policy stakeholders. The two spheres of work merged, and we planned a gathering at the district level in

Kailahun, where we could both convene a dialogue and share the Kissi Teng People's Plan, including the process used to facilitate it.

We were explicit from the start about the goal of the gathering. We wanted to invite the full cross-section of district leaders to reflect on lessons of the postwar recovery process and apply them to the post-Ebola response period. We wanted those reflections to be grounded in local perspectives and communities' lived experiences, and we wanted everyone together to imagine the kind of post-Ebola response and recovery they most wanted to see, and how they wanted to bring their own leadership to it.

And so, in July of 2015, Fambul Tok and Catalyst for Peace partnered with Kailahun's District Ebola Response Committee to convene all of the district-level Ebola response and development stakeholders—a gathering that, improbable as it may sound, was the first of its kind. Participants included the district council and district officer; traditional leaders (paramount chiefs); relevant national government ministries, departments, and agencies based at the district level; national and international NGOs; the WHO and other international actors in the Ebola response; community members; representatives of traditionally underrepresented population groups, including the disabled, women, and youth; and Muslim and Christian leaders.

At the center of the gathering were twenty people from Kissi Teng Chiefdom who presented their Chiefdom People's Plan and described, in their own words, the process and the impact of creating it. Many had never been to Kailahun Town or interacted with the levels of leadership represented at this conference. They electrified the gathering with their energy and spirit, and with the details of their plan and their description of its creation process. "We want to be the ones to determine our needs, and we want to support the larger efforts in our chiefdom," an early speaker noted, and others reiterated. They committed to facilitating conflict resolution within their communities, increasing community education on Ebola prevention, improving health-care delivery services, strengthening farming, and growing local and regional agricultural markets.

Among the 20 people who spoke that day was a local section chief who recounted a meeting with an NGO offering to "help" his community by bringing its project there. Though he hadn't asked for that "help," he said he didn't think back then that he could say no. Standing taller, he noted that now he knew that he could say no if what the NGO was planning wasn't what they wanted. "I will show them our People's Plan," he said with obvious pride, "and say that if they really want to help, they could look at this first to see what we want and need." Heads nodded across the room as he spoke, and there was an eruption of side conversations, especially among the group of paramount chiefs, about how that kind of thing happened in their chiefdoms all the time. The response was so energetic that the community presentation had to be momentarily paused.

Prior to the Kissi Teng's group presentation of their People's Plan, their paramount chief, the traditional leader given utmost respect in Sierra Leone, had ceremonially presented the document to the local government officials. In most official settings, even in a gathering like ours, with 20 people present from the villages across his chiefdom, his voice would have been the only communal voice heard. Paramount chiefs are treated with such deference that it is common for their subjects simply to sit silently in their presence. In that context, going beyond the ceremonial to have vocal and vigorous cross-community involvement in the presentation of the People's

Plan, not to mention the full participation of all 20 representatives throughout the whole gathering, already spoke volumes—as did the fact that their paramount chief invited and encouraged it. This engagement would repeat in other chiefdoms and districts, as if the PPP were calling forth a new kind of leadership, not just from ordinary citizens but from those with more formal leadership roles. A year later, for example, when the paramount chief of Fakunya Chiefdom officially presented their People's Plan to the Moyamba District Council, he explained he hadn't realized how much his subjects were actually capable of until he saw the energy and skill and commitment they brought to the PPP. "Now I feel like *they're* leading *me!*" he said.

Kailahun District leaders at that first conference were impressed by the powerful living example of what happens when space is created and held for communities, and they affirmed a strong desire to use the PPP for the district's post-Ebola response, rolling the process out across every chiefdom. Though it was difficult for many of the NGOs and INGOs to hear, the traditional leaders and local government leaders spoke frankly about their experiences with NGOs imposing their own agendas, which often had little to do with locals' needs. They expressed their desire for a stronger platform for them to define their own needs and lead from that basis. Like the section chief from Kissi Teng, they, too, were realizing that they could actually say no to aid that they felt was being imposed on them, and that they could help shape a different kind of recovery and development process for their district.

There was broad recognition that such an inclusive gathering opened up possibilities for frank conversation and creative imagining for the district that might not have been possible otherwise. Fambul

Tok had plans to expand the PPP pilot to Koinadugu and Moyamba Districts. Their Ebola response committee leaders were also at the Kailahun meeting, and both called on Fambul Tok to bring the PPP to their districts, paving the way for Fambul Tok to deepen its early work. Once the PPP had been completed across an entire chiefdom in each new district, similar district stakeholder gatherings were held in Koinadugu and Moyamba with the same goals in mind: coming together to learn the lessons offered by the postwar recovery and to envision and plan for the kind of post-Ebola process they most wanted to experience.

Just as the PPP had invited villagers to identify their needs and how they desired to meet them, the district stakeholder gatherings did the same for local government leaders. Those leading development in the district described the problems with the way things had usually been done—problems rooted in broken relationships among the various district stakeholders and their feeling of disrespect or lack of support from national and international actors. When invited to think about how they wanted to do things differently, the district stakeholders identified a need for a place to come together and collaborate in an ongoing way.

From this was born the Inclusive District Committee, or IDC for short. In the three pilot districts, Fambul Tok facilitated the IDCs in choosing their compositions and mandates, identifying their core values, and creating the organizational structures they would need. The IDCs wanted to see the PPP cascade across the chiefdoms in their districts, and they began building linkages between what communities wanted and the services that would support them.

Truly, this was democracy in action.

Sometimes, people just need to be invited

One of the most powerful examples of this work in action was in the village of Kpoundu, in Kissi Teng Chiefdom—more specifically, in Fatim Sesay herself. Fatim was a Peace Mother in Kissi Teng and one of roughly two dozen people chosen to represent the chiefdom at the district stakeholders conference in Kailahun Town. Now, back in her village, she was sharing what she'd heard at the conference with her fellow Peace Mothers.

She stood tall and confident, arms extended for emphasis, in front of the women, sitting in a semicircle beneath the mango trees. The bright-red-and-white circles on Fatim's wrapped lapa skirt, paired with a short-sleeve, black-and-white shirt, gave her a youthful informality. But her words demonstrated both a sophisticated understanding and a powerful capacity to communicate as she narrated the events of the district stakeholders' meeting. Her language was accessible and without jargon, yet she also communicated the significance of an event that had national and even international import.

Connecting the opportunity at hand with the core message from the stakeholders' conference, she assured the women gathered that July day that their voices as women were key to their communities' recovery, and that the PPP wanted them to lead. She reminded them that they had the power to begin their own recovery process without having to wait for anyone's help or permission, and that they could accomplish a great deal by working together. And then Fatim invited them to do just that.

The women immediately jumped into organizing their plans. They wanted to work together and earn money to begin addressing myriad community needs, as they prioritized them, and the work began that very moment.

John and I watched from the edges of the group as the meeting unfolded, impressed with Fatim's articulate delivery and her ability to invite the women to step into their own power and agency to act on behalf of their communities.

"Wow, you should snap her up for the Fambul Tok staff!" I whispered to John, just as he was turning toward me, about to say the same thing. Fambul Tok operated that way in many instances—looking for people in the community who both embodied and communicated the program values skillfully, and then inviting and training them to take on leadership positions.

We didn't know at the time the extent to which that had already happened with Fatim, shepherded by Lilian Morsay, the national coordinator of the Peace Mothers program. Lilian had been helping to lead the PPP pilot in Kailahun District and to launch the Peace Mothers program in Kissi Teng Chiefdom. She'd noticed the same talents in Fatim that John and I had, and she approached Fatim to help run an early-stage community-planning meeting. But Fatim had never played a public leadership role—a reality not uncommon for rural women in Sierra Leone—and at first, she literally ran from Lilian and hid inside her house. Lilian coaxed her out of hiding, encouraging and reassuring her several times before Fatim was willing to step forward. And step forward she did. With Lilian's support, she blossomed. Her potential became realized, and her informal leadership grew into something more formalized and structured as her community asked her to represent them in more and more ways.

Lilian had sensed Fatim's potential and invited her to step into it more fully, supporting and encouraging her along the way. The same had happened to Lilian herself, whose leadership capacity had been seen and acknowledged from her earliest days with Fambul Tok, supported by John and other staff into fuller and stronger expression. Lilian had been featured in a short documentary on the Peace Mothers a couple of years before the meeting in Kpoundu, and she spoke so naturally and powerfully that she anchored the impact of the film. I still remember the day I first showed it to the staff after we had just finished it. Upon seeing herself on the big screen and hearing how the film was already making its way around the world to great acclaim, Lilian was stunned into silence. She couldn't speak the rest of the day. I learned from her later that seeing this film showed her the powerful ways she could be a leader—and in fact, that she already was. She began to step more eagerly into program leadership roles and embraced more and more responsibility. She made it her mission to mentor others, especially other women. She knew from experience the power of being "invited out"—and given space to unfurl and unfold, to blossom into full voice, activity, and capacity. And she had a rock-solid commitment to paying it forward and helping others, especially women, step into their full capacity as leaders.

Lilian had done just that for Fatim, without fanfare. And John and I were now continuing the process. We saw and recognized Fatim's spirit and skill, and John invited it into further action and expression, bringing Fatim on as a Fambul Tok district staff member. After a short time on staff, she asked to help facilitate the People's Planning Process in a new district, stepping up to a national role. Meanwhile, she was also appointed by her community and became an active and respected leader of Kailahun's new Inclusive District Committee. In early 2018, she went with a small group of Fambul Tok Peace Mothers and staff to a global women's peacebuilding leadership retreat in Kenya, where her story inspired women across Africa and the United States.

It's not always easy to grow. Fatim's skills were not readily recognized, at least not using the common metrics of the established aid and development system. But the People's Planning Process subverts those norms by actively seeking potential at the most local level and building infrastructure out from there, step by step. The word "infrastructure" is misleading, as the essence of the work is not mechanical but personal and human. It is *relationships* that enliven and empower each part of that infrastructure—invitational relationships rooted in care and connection. Fambul Tok staff reach out to encourage and support community leaders throughout the process in practical, ongoing ways. This ongoing and highly human connection and care from "the outside" is like warm sunshine or a gentle rain on a parched field. It invites the seeds softened in the fallow ground to germinate. Paired with the committee structures, it beckons emerging leaders to burst forth into green shoots, sturdy saplings, and eventually rooted trees to anchor their communities.

The foundational activity in helping people and communities realize their potential is extending the invitation—*inviting* someone to step into a leadership role. So many people are capable of so much, if they are only *asked*. But too often, they go unasked, uninvited. The power of that invitation is amplified by positive mirroring, as when Lilian reflected back to Fatim the qualities and capabilities she was seeing, which helped Fatim express them in even greater ways—just as we had seen the Peace Mothers film serve as a positive mirror for Lilian, helping her see her capacities in the larger context in a way she hadn't before.

There's a magic that happens when an outsider sees untapped

potential and invites it into fuller expression. When that person is also consciously growing more fully into *their* leadership capacity, supported by people and a community external but connected to them, the magnifying power for positive growth is exponentially enhanced. It becomes like a positive spiral, and the breathtaking power of seeing others blossom serves to invite, inspire, and empower us all to do the same. In this framework, all are part of a living organism, an organism that, like a tree, is growing toward the light.

Chapter 14

REPAIRING THE CUP

Once organized, the Inclusive District Committees were as eager as the Kissi Teng Peace Mothers to get to work. The IDCs immediately developed a cyclical process of identifying priority issues in their district, planning how they wanted to address them and implementing their plans. In their first year alone, the IDCs addressed outbreaks or threats of violence, especially in connection with the national elections and youth disenfranchisement, and they more actively monitored the implementation and quality of national projects in their districts, among other initiatives. They also began addressing long-standing conflicts between and among district stakeholders, building a collaborative capacity whose absence had previously hampered the success of everyone's efforts.

This capacity was tested by deep, long-standing conflict between local councils and traditional leaders, which quickly emerged as a priority issue for each IDC. The two governance bodies are meant to be the twin engines of local development, but their relationship had been eroded by years of suspicion and mistrust, in particular about the collection and use of tax revenue. The challenge crystallized first in Kailahun District, at the beginning of the IDC formation process, when conflict over revenue collection had become so entrenched that the paramount chiefs were threatening strikes, protests, and even violence if district officials dared to come to their chiefdoms to collect taxes. It quickly became clear that the heart of the problem was not money or territory but communication. A lack of transparency was experienced in both directions as a lack of accountability.

Fambul Tok invited the sides to dialogue and played a facilitation and accompaniment role. The paramount chiefs and the district councils met four times to express their grievances and to find a way forward. The process was lengthy and not without difficulty, but in the end, it worked. An agreement was signed.

It became possible to address even long-standing difficult issues because the IDCs, like the more local CWMCs, created a space for all the stakeholders to see themselves as part of a common "we." The district bowl was becoming as visible as the community bowl. And the IDC offered a structure and process for the district to repair the cracks in its own bowl.

The iterative, cyclical nature of this new phase of Fambul Tok's work was becoming clear: inviting local planning and action led to establishing local infrastructure to implement, support, and sustain that action, which then led to building and connecting to the next level of infrastructure to ensure that progress went forward . . . in order to invite the next level of planning and action. As that cycle unfurled itself, a more whole and healthy system was emerging, in practice.

The bottle and the cup

At events like the Kailahun District Stakeholders Conference, I usually played a behind-the-scenes role, but for this event, Catalyst for Peace was publicly listed as a co-convener, and I was on the agenda as a speaker. I wanted to help make visible our core concepts, the ideas that both grounded and gave shape and direction to our work, and in turn to help give language and framing for a community-centered approach to the recovery process.

As I accompanied Fambul Tok's emergence over the years, one of my roles was often to reflect back what I was seeing and hearing. In my presentation, I took John's metaphor of the community as a cracked bowl and turned it into a live demonstration, using the imagery to reflect back the powerful wisdom of local knowledge. With the materials at hand, the bowl became a "cup." I sawed off the tops of two water bottles, and I cut holes in the bottom of one. I called that cup the community and explained how the cup itself was invisible in the aid system.

Then I lifted a full water bottle, which represented aid as it usually worked. That aid, like the water, was poured into the community to address a problem or crisis—and of course, in my demonstration, the water spilled right through. The room came alive. Everybody immediately understood that the cup couldn't hold water because it was cracked. And everybody understood exactly what that meant in their context. Because the water didn't solve the problem, I noted that those bringing the aid felt like they had to keep pouring more water in. But it was clear that water alone *couldn't* solve the problem—and in fact often made the cracks worse, all the while depleting the water in the bottle, creating an unhealthy cycle and leaving everyone worse off.

I described how Fambul Tok's work wasn't about pouring water in, but about repairing the cup. And then for good measure, I took the cup with no cracks and poured water in, and of course it filled right up.

Humanitarian aid is like water; the community is like a cup. If that cup is cracked, any water poured in goes right through.

The metaphor spoke so well to people working across all sectors that I have done the same demonstration in every presentation I've made since about the PPP and the approach it embodied. At a meeting nearly four years later, I reconnected with one of the district leaders from Kailahun who had been at that initial meeting. He gave me a warm hello and, with a smile of recognition, proclaimed, "You're the cup lady!" Fambul Tok staff adopted the demonstration as part of their training in communities, using it to illustrate the core work of the People's Planning Process, and it is now part of the common vocabulary of any community that has been a part of the PPP.

From straight line to nested bowls

Making visible the community container in social change work is critical to the work of repairing its cracks. The demonstration and metaphor also expose other characteristics of the usual aid system, namely an assumed separation between those giving and those receiving, and the consequent dichotomization of aid—those with resources (whether money or ideas) on one side and those with needs on the other. That makes it much more difficult to see, let alone to invite and receive, the resources communities already have, including their potential to lead, plan, and enact change for themselves. It perpetuates a limited view of what constitutes both resources and needs.

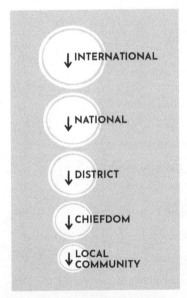

In a hierarchical, top-down, or outside-in system, sectors are fragmented and largely act on each other.

In this framing, the flow of resources and support, whether it comes from the chiefdom, district, national, or international level, is inherently one-way. It moves from the outside in, from the bottle to the cup. By dichotomizing resources and needs, an outside-in system de facto keeps them from coming together, creating cycles of codependency and depletion. The sectors in this system are all fragmented, and largely acting *upon* each other. The phrase "top-down" is often used to describe this system, which illuminates the hierarchy embedded in the framework.

The implication of the language of "top-down" is that if you don't like it or if you want to change it, the alternative is "bottom-up." But that language also perpetuates the assumption of hierarchy, and it doesn't challenge the original assumption of separation and fragmentation.

That is not the framework we were envisioning or living into.

In our work, we have envisioned the international aid system as **nested circles**, with local communities in the center. In this configuration, roles are distinct, but there is no hierarchy. Rather, the role of each sector, of each ring in the circle, is to hold and invite and support the purpose and potential of those within it, and to share ideas and learning with the circles outside it. This allows for a two-way flow of resources—including from the inside out. Each level has distinct roles, resources, and needs, but all work together as part of a larger whole.

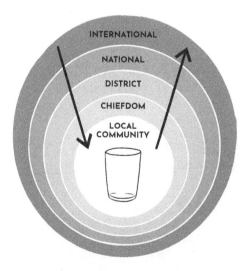

In an inside-out framework, communities are at the center. Sectors have distinct locations, roles, resources, and needs, and all work together as part of a larger whole.

That phrase bears repeating: *as part of a larger whole.* In our work over the years with Fambul Tok, including now in this new phase of our partnership with them supporting the People's Planning Process and an inclusive governance process, we were operating from an understanding of the system *as an interconnected whole.* Even with Catalyst's status as a funder, we located ourselves as part of and within that larger, interconnected whole and shaped our role and work accordingly. We were holding that understanding of a whole, healthy, interconnected system in an already-not-yet way, acting *from* it while also actively working toward it through our partnership with Fambul Tok, bringing this system into fuller manifestation in an incremental way.

Over time, I've come to prefer a three-dimensional imaging of this theory, sparked by an everyday item in my very own kitchen— nested bowls:

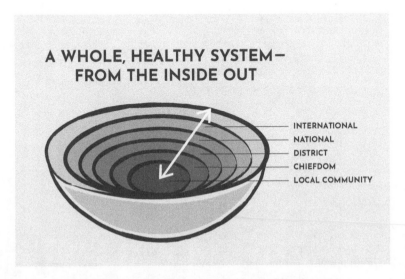

A WHOLE, HEALTHY SYSTEM—
FROM THE INSIDE OUT

INTERNATIONAL
NATIONAL
DISTRICT
CHIEFDOM
LOCAL COMMUNITY

The international system as nested bowls.

In the earliest part of the PPP, Fambul Tok helped repair the cracks in the local community bowl by bringing together village representatives for honest, neighbor-to-neighbor conversation about their needs, goals, challenges, and desires—holding space for frank talk, even about difficult things. By inviting collective action, and by establishing structures like the Peace Mothers and the CWMCs to support and engage that action, the local community bowl was repaired. The Inclusive Chiefdom Committees and the process that established them repaired the chiefdom bowl, which then allowed the chiefdom to better support the local communities (the next bowl in) and also to better advocate to the district (the next bowl out). Similarly, the Inclusive District Committees repaired the district bowl, allowing districts to lead their own peace and development more effectively, both to better support the chiefdoms that supported the local communities (sections and villages) and to better advocate for people's needs at the national level.

You get the picture.

In this set of bowls, the largest one is not labeled. I think of that outside bowl as representing the very idea of wholeness, of a whole, healthy, regenerative system, in whatever places and ways it might be manifest or in motion. That is the ultimate container that holds us all, and it has held John and me as we have taken each step forward in our work together. It showed up as the inner voice I heard tapping my consciousness, saying, "It doesn't have to be that way"—a voice calling forward the *idea* of a mutually healthy, whole system. John and I listened to and for that idea in each step of our Ebola response, and it guided us not only to launch a national policy dialogue but also to begin to build and model that system starting at the most local level.

This larger idea, the very idea of already-not-yet wholeness, holds us all. It invites us all to see how it is present and alive as well as how it can be made (more) manifest. It invites us to locate ourselves within it, grounding in it, right here and now, wherever else in the system we may see ourselves or our work. Centering and grounding ourselves within an inside-out system asks something of us—that we listen and learn and align ourselves, our relationships, and our actions accordingly. My hope is that seeing this kind of system made visible, both in concept and in practice, makes it easier for us to do just that. How can each of us, right where we are located, listen for and live into that more healthy and whole system? How can we work to repair the communal containers that hold us? How can we align our work and our relationships more fully with the values of mutuality, of hearing to speech, and of sharing fully and freely what we're learning?

And what is possible when we do?

Chapter 15

GROWING THE WE

A s the work of Catalyst for Peace and Fambul Tok shifted and grew in response to the needs in Sierra Leone, I was able to bring my ongoing vision and leadership because I was on a similar journey individually, and Catalyst for Peace was on a parallel journey organizationally. The organization, and the individuals leading it, were also growing into a new, emerging, strengthening **we**.

My Wisdom Circle had held space for my deepening as a person and as a leader, for discerning the next level of how Catalyst for Peace was meant to work in the world, and for identifying what capacity and strengthening we would need organizationally to live into that. It felt critical to integrate those wisdom-tuning conversations more directly into CFP's work—in fact, to acknowledge them as a core part *of* our work. The Wisdom Circle had become a channel for my connection to the outermost bowl, that very concept of a system of wholeness that also supported my individual wholeness. This was a channel I felt we were meant to hold open more widely—for ourselves organizationally and for the system emerging in practice in Sierra Leone. Naming and holding that connection was actually an essential contribution.

So in 2015, I hired Amy and Charles, the two people at the heart of my Wisdom Circle, and together we brought the circle *inside* the organization. Their addition marked a transition for me from thinking about Catalyst's leadership as an "I" to seeing it as a "we"—a "we" that included me but was also bigger than me. I had been yearning for an expanded leadership team, and I trusted these changes would bring greater strength and co-creative capacity for our work in Sierra Leone, as well as for moving into the opportunities calling us internationally. Yet I also felt the resistance that accompanies change. In holding sole leadership for Catalyst over the years, I had honed my independence and, with it, fierce protectiveness of our work and process, qualities that had emboldened us to work in innovative ways. While I knew I still needed those capacities, I also knew we were being called into a bigger space. And I knew that moving into that bigger space would require both personal and organizational growth. In one of our last Wisdom Circle meetings, I described feeling "rootbound," knowing I needed a bigger container in order to stretch out my roots and grow.

The expanded team gathered in Harrisonburg, Virginia, in June of 2015 for our first staff retreat, marking these multiple transitions. Although opening to the new, we were not starting over, and I needed to feel that we were building from the integrity of the strong foundation we already had. We all felt that looking *back* together on CFP's history was an important foundation for looking *forward* together. We unfurled a roll of blank butcher paper over end-to-end tables in the middle of the room, and on it we crafted a "river" of the history of CFP's work in the world—not merely an abstract timeline but an expression of the organization as a living entity, an idea with its own life and flow. This newly visible whole, and the metaphor of a river itself, showed us how new programming and new leadership adds new momentum, like a confluence, and strengthens the river's integrity on its inexorable flow from source to destination. It also revealed the ways Amy and Charles had each flowed in and out of our work and story over the years.

I also wanted the expanded team to be grounded in the full scope of our current programming and materials, to be fully "inside" CFP's present. I had brought our book, our films, our educational manual, and representations of all of our other work and programs, and I mounted them on the walls around the room. We spent the rest of the afternoon going through each one. It did indeed bring us together into the fullness of the present moment, and I think we all felt a deep appreciation for the richness of what was there.

I was energized by all of this during the day, but after dinner, I felt impelled to come back into the room and just be there by myself. I sat quietly, overwhelmed by how cramped and inadequate the space felt now, as if the walls were closing in on me. The space was too full, leaving no space for new creation. Being in it exhausted me.

In that moment, I was overcome by a full and complete *not-knowing*. I simply had no idea what to do next, at the very moment I felt we were being called to move forward into the world more boldly. I also sensed that the *way of being*, and of leading, that had brought forward everything represented around me was now too small for me. It may have guided us to that point, but it no longer worked for what was calling us forward. But I didn't know how to break out of it. It was like the river of CFP's work in the world, and of my leadership, had reached a dam. The pressure was building, but at this moment, in this place . . . *we were stuck.*

And we still had three more days to go.

I felt alone and despondent, and I could only muster a despairing prayer, more like a humble statement of fact, that if we were going to go forward with a renewed purpose, someone else was going to have to step forward and open the way. A big part of me felt like that meant I was failing in my leadership. I eventually made an uneasy truce with not knowing and got a fitful night's sleep.

The next morning, I dragged my empty-feeling self back to our meeting room and found a delightful surprise. The tables that held the CFP "river" had been moved down the room, and another table had been added at the end. The roll of butcher paper now extended out another six feet over this new table, a delightfully blank expanse of possibility opening into the future.

I burst into a huge smile. "We have a future! We have new possibility!" I sang inside. And I didn't have to take sole responsibility for making it happen!

Charles had been impelled to open up more space during the night, and he had spent a good deal of time searching for another table. He ended up shifting all of the furniture to be able to add it at the end. A simple gesture at one level, yet in that moment it transformed my consciousness and countenance. It was an embodied experience of us moving into a larger, more open space—the space of the unknown, of new possibility, and ultimately of co-creativity.

And *I* didn't have to create the way. I didn't have to move forward all on my own. I didn't have to "figure it all out."

Moving into a larger space isn't easy. As simple as it sounds when we name it, the reality is that when we are pushing the boundaries of our own internal learning, the work of letting go of what no longer serves and opening to receive something new is hard, hard, hard. It is not just outer work—physically changing the space or building something new. It is also inner work. And oftentimes the qualities we cultivate for success in one space are the very qualities we need to moderate, release, or hold differently in order to cross the threshold to the next.

At our retreat, we worked hard to understand what was on the other side of that threshold for Catalyst for Peace. As part of our vision of growing the practice of inside-out peace and development globally, we remained committed to supporting the work in Sierra Leone and helping it grow. We knew that in order to hold space for the new work emerging in there—to continue to hold the national bowl—we would have to grow and strengthen our *own* bowl. We wanted to see the PPP expand nationally, but Catalyst didn't have the money to finance that. We also knew a national expansion would require political buy-in and close partnership with the national government, which we had so far avoided. Securing large-scale funding and national political engagement is fraught with pressure to bend to others' needs, interests, or demands. It can feel like there's no choice but to compromise core principles in order to secure and preserve needed resources or support. We needed to be strong enough at our core that we could help find that support for Fambul Tok's new phase of work while also helping them—and us—stay aligned to our core purposes and values. We needed more connection and flow with the outermost bowl—the wisdom of wholeness itself, and of the ways it resourced us—in order to help channel its flow to the work that was emerging in Sierra Leone. That required a strong, and ever-strengthening, *we*.

It also required us as leaders and as Catalyst for Peace to be more present and visible. It wasn't that we felt a need to be more visible in Sierra Leone for visibility's sake. We were trying to make the role of the international partner an explicit part of the crisis-recovery conversation, to shine a critical light on unconscious assumptions about the relationship between national and international actors, still rooted in colonial dynamics of separation and control, and to live out better alternatives. We wanted to model a more invitational partnership grounded in a relationship of mutuality, and we wanted to invite others into the same. We wanted to make a healthy, whole system visible by both living it out and voicing it, and by inviting other international actors into a new paradigm that supports people and communities, *all* people and communities, in fulfilling their potential.

Having unblocked the Catalyst dam, I had assumed the river would flow forward, wider and stronger. Instead, we saw that we were not even in a river at all. We were actually in a large, open space—a space with wide and far shores that received and gently calmed all of the pent-up pressure from the dam. We needed, wanted, and claimed a "lake" as the space that held this next phase of flow. Without the throes of a current, we could open to this time of stillness and depth, of space for reflection. In the wide open, we could go deep. We honored our space for reflection in everything we did together, and we discovered a surprising power in that collective depth, an integrative power, and a wellspring of replenishment and inspiration. This "lake time," as we called it (noticing with pleasure the way our initials together—Libby, Amy, Charles—also suggested that naming), helped us lean into and rest in the principles and ideas that grounded and called and held us— our outermost bowl. Creating space for *the work of creating space* requires this kind of powerful surrender to what holds and nourishes us and our purpose. And that's what we committed to living and learning our way into.

Wombing and being wombed

Though little acknowledged in the arena of social and political change, the work of holding space for something new to emerge is actually a basic—perhaps *the* most basic—biological activity. We all came into this world having grown from a tiny cell into an infant inside our mother's womb. Naming "wombing" as a verb helps us see how the work of holding space represents so much more than passively placing a boundary around something. Wombing provides a temporary home—a space of direct nourishment and emergence—for a new idea or entity to grow and develop until it is ready to spring into fuller expression and independent integrity. Wombs are, of course, completely comfortable with not knowing, with the emergence-in-process of what's meant to be. The womb can't "engineer" what's inside it; all it can do is provide hospitable conditions for nurturing the growth and development of what it holds. And inevitably there comes a time when the womb is too small for the infant inside it. At that point, baby and mother work together to push the baby into a new, bigger space—the home for its next phase of growth. I don't want to take the metaphor too literally or too far. And yet, it feels important to state the obvious: that this is the most basic, the most human, work in the world—to hold space for something that does not yet exist visibly and help it bring itself into expression.

Expanding CFP's core leadership team by bringing my Wisdom Circle, the place that so effectively and nourishingly held *me* as a person and as a leader, into our organizational core made it possible for CFP to become more visible at a crucial moment in the work we shared with Fambul Tok. That visibility was key to our new mission, not only to help birth a new way of working in Sierra Leone but also to model a system we believed all of us could work in—a whole, healthy system where each of us could be present and lead from our whole selves, in mutual relationship with one another.

To see this, I had to learn that being part of a larger whole requires a kind of surrender, first to the work of helping call forth and create a trustworthy organizational container and then to leaning into and resting in—abiding in—that container. Growing a wombing system necessitates not just a commitment to creating wombing spaces but a willingness to *be wombed*—to be held and nourished in a deliberate way, in all our *own* emergence and in-process-ness, and to emerge from that space when it is too small for us. It requires trusting the forces of both wombing and birthing—and the care and tending that will come after birth. None of this would have been possible without this new growth for CFP, a growth that we consciously cultivated from our very core.

Thinking about strengthening our core opens the question: "Core of *what*?" *Where* we imagine ourselves located is actually critical. I have learned that we can bring conscious choice to that imagining. It is hard for me to put words to it, but in my clumsy language I would say that core to my spiritual journey and practice has been more and more consciously locating myself—grounding myself, centering and seeing myself—as already within a system that is whole and healthy. When I am able to inhabit that space in consciousness, to imagine myself already in a healthy and whole system, and I bring that consciousness to whatever work I am doing, I have felt able to sense the next unfolding expression of that system I am being called to support, to help manifest.

This sensing and centering is a fundamentally spiritual act, since any "system" isn't usually visible, and we rarely explicitly consider our assumptions about the kind of system we're inhabiting or where we've located ourselves within it. Like any spiritual act, this centering also requires a kind of humility, a depth of vulnerability—a willingness to inhabit the unknown with faith and trust.

Having trusted companions on this journey, having and being in community, has been critical for my learning and practice of this. I have also found collective, communal reflection, discernment, and imagination to be something distinctly different from the solo variety, and powerfully generative. There's a kind of discernment we can do with others, together, that's different from what we can do on our own.

There's a deep lesson in that for me about all the ways I, and we, need others. I've come to see how needing others actually increases our power—that the willingness to be met and to *be held* by others, to be wombed, is actually a critical power in social change. The willingness to stand in the middle of the unknown, to see what we need, to invite and invoke it—and then to receive it and to trust. Listening and trusting, and then acting from that space of trust, draws into our life people, ideas, and processes that have great gifts for us. Those acts of faith do as much, if not more, to catalyze outward social change as any direct, externally driven, accomplishment-oriented activity.

And yet the power of our limitations, of our vulnerability, is not recognized or taught. I can't remember a single class, seminar, or training I ever took—academic, professional, or personal—that invited me to increase my power through cultivating my willingness and ability to need others. Even writing that sounds absurd. In fact, the primary message I've received throughout my life has been just the opposite, especially in international peace and security, and those were the ideas that fed my lone-wolf leadership tendencies. I've had to unlearn and learn, over and over again, to make new mental grooves—an often painful and certainly long, and long-term, process.

Over the years, I've observed a rhythm emerge between wombing and being wombed. When I don't try and rush, when I don't force a solely outward focus, but instead allow what's in me to gestate as needed—then my, and our, commitments to support *others'* emergence into their own potential unfold in a more balanced way. When you're part of a living organism, it makes sense that there is a living rhythm to this interplay.

And that's just it. I have been living into and out from an image of the international system as a living organism. Individually, I've had to learn to listen to and respect the needs of my body in order to better discern, ask for, and accept what I need. It's almost as if I've also, and in parallel, been learning to listen to and for the needs of the collective living body I'm part of, of the system that wants to be manifest, as it goes forward and grows in and through our actions. That healthy, whole system is, at some level, already here. And it wants to be seen and inhabited, right here, right now. It is present, in all its already-not-yet glory, and we can help it grow.

Just bloom

Nearing the end of that Harrisonburg retreat, as thrilled as I was to have grown from an I to a we, I was also acutely aware that I didn't have much lived experience of leading from that place, as a part of a *we*.

How would I do it? *Could* I even do it? And were we really going to be able to step into this next phase of work with more strength and grace, actually offering to the world all that we knew we had to offer? I could feel the familiar burdensome sense of responsibility knocking once more on the doors of my consciousness.

I carried the questions and accompanying feelings of anxiety with me as we moved into a break. Heading out for a walk around the beautiful grounds, I resolved to hold them lightly, with trust and gentle listening.

I wasn't far into my walk when I stumbled into a large stand of bright orange daylilies, practically dancing with extraordinary color. I drew my breath in and stopped to admire them, exclaiming out loud at their stunning beauty. "Oh! You're SOOO beautiful! Thank you!" I gushed. "Thank you for blooming!" I stood there for a long while, my open-mouthed smile as wide as my face as I simply delighted in the gift of this gorgeousness.

And then it struck me. Just as I was spontaneously spilling out love for the unforced beauty of these lilies, that same kind of love was available to and for *me*—for all of us—right at that very moment. An infinite and unbounded Love was present to and for me, astounded at my beauty, in love with my uniqueness, and spilling over gratitude for all the depth and color of my being, bursting into glorious expression. "You are SOOO beautiful!" I could hear that Love telling me. And I knew I could—and needed to—receive the benediction: "Thank you for blooming!" As I did, I realized the guidance I needed for the work ahead.

Ahh. Just bloom!

I could receive and bathe in the same words that I heard spilling out of my mouth at the sight of these flowers. I felt a sense of the larger, divine Soul that was just as surely expressing itself in the work of Fambul Tok and Catalyst for Peace as it was through these daylilies. It was all the handiwork of the same divine Love, which was breathing through it all—the burst of glorious bloom, the awe at the beauty, the willingness to *be* beauty in the world, and the love and appreciation and gratitude for *all* the blooming beauty, including my own, and our own, expression of it. And the feeling and forwarding of the invitation to all flowering things— simply to bloom.

This insight brought me back to how I'd felt hearing John's answer to the question of how to respond to the volunteer who had stolen funds from the community: "I don't know, but together we'll figure it out." He had opened my thought to see the very practical ways that the larger whole holds us, and that it is trustworthy. That we can trust what we are working to express in the world to be in operation on our behalf. My encounter with the lilies was showing me the same thing, in different language. I received the message gratefully, feeling the freedom and the invitation to move forward into the unknown with more faith and grace.

I knew this message was for us organizationally as well. Our newly strengthened *we* could see and lean into the trusted whole that was bigger than us but also included us, knowing it was in operation on our behalf, even in the middle of all the unknowns.

Part V

THE WHOLE MADE VISIBLE

Chapter 16

UNFOLDING AND UNFURLING

I couldn't understand a word she said, but I think she might have communicated more than anyone else at the conference.

Musu Mohammed is from Semabu, a village in Peje Bongre Chiefdom in Kailahun District. She couldn't read or write, and she had never held a formal leadership role or title, but none of this kept her from being a powerful leader and communicator. Her village had selected her, as someone they respected and trusted to hold their community's interests at heart, to represent them in the People's Planning Process a few months earlier, and then she was selected to represent the eight villages in her section in meetings at the chiefdom level.

Now, at the Taiama Conference Center in southern Sierra Leone, the paramount chief officially presented the Peje Bongre Chiefdom People's Plan to the Kailahun District Council chairman, with Musu and a group of 15 or so others from the chiefdom standing alongside him. Chosen as the spokesperson for the group, Musu shared with conference delegates how the plan had been developed and what it meant to them. As she spoke, she transformed from a tiny, frail-looking woman into the very definition of embodied power—and she transformed the room with her.

She spoke in Mende, her tribal language, with a breathless energy that left no time for the customary translations, into either Krio or English. But translations were hardly necessary. She owned the room, and she did so with unassuming naturalness. She was literally surrounded by local and national government officials, even the minister of local government and rural development himself, and other leaders from across Sierra Leone, Africa, and the world. She communicated with crystal clarity—even to those who couldn't understand her words—that her voice was at the *center* of the event. She infused the space with the power of her and her community's further potential—its own already-not-yet strength. It would have been impossible to hear her speak about her chiefdom's accomplishments and ambitions and to conclude that what she outlined was impossible, or to resist the pull to do more yourself to ensure that it all got actualized.

Sensing the system that wants to spring forth

Musu's presentation was part of a national conference that Fambul Tok and Catalyst for Peace convened to grow the people-led planning and development work beyond its pilot. In November of 2016, we gathered the executives of the three pilot IDCs, who now had a solid year of experience under their belts, for the first Inter-District Learning (IDL) Conference, an event dedicated to helping them share with and learn from each other and build webs of connection between the districts. In addition, we wanted to build the foundation for a national platform that could spread the process across the country, and we wanted that foundation to be fully grounded in the distilled experience from the local and district leaders. To support a national platform, we wanted to invite the national-level leaders and government officials who would need to be involved for it to succeed. We also wanted to share the already substantial body of experience from three districts with a global audience, hoping to open channels for multidirectional learning.

We wanted to accomplish all of those goals—strengthening district leadership, beginning to build a national platform, and opening global learning channels—using a conference process that embodied the community centeredness of both the work and the listening presence it takes to support and amplify that work. Community members who had completed the PPP presented directly about the process and the plan they created through it, rather than having a staff member or district officer describe it on their behalf. That's why the Peje Bongre delegation was attending and presenting their newly completed People's Plan at the conference instead of waiting to announce it at the usual district council or IDC meeting in their district.

To begin the gathering, John and I walked delegates through the history and process of the PPP and the IDCs and introduced the core concepts of an inside-out approach. When Musu spoke, the power and potential of those ideas took on an embodied reality. It was almost as if the alignment of the room shifted. The group was no longer divided into practitioners, presenters, and observers;

we were now all *participants* in a larger whole—a system of practice and learning with people and communities in the center.

The nested circles of the inside-out framework also came to life. In the room, we had an international contingent, observing from the edges, who encircled national leaders from both government and civil society, who encircled district government and IDC leaders, who encircled the community activists who were living out the People's Planning Process. The PPP had repaired the cracks in the Peje Bongre community bowl, and Musu's words and presence showed how full that bowl had become—full of the community's own ideas, energy, and commitment. Those of us in outer circles, or bowls, felt how that energy and inspiration could actually flow out and resource *us*.

Musu's words and presence, in the context of the conference, invited us all to see and feel ourselves as part of a larger whole, a system that invited and supported and honored and channeled the best from people and communities, in service of that larger whole. And *that* was something that spoke to the deepest yearnings of everyone there, even if inchoately. Over the next days, what was inchoate would become more consciously named and claimed.

Scaling up—from the inside out

When Maya Moiwo Kai-Kai, then Sierra Leone's minister of local government, gave his address, I was stunned and thrilled to hear him say, "This is exactly what we need, and what my ministry wants to and is supposed to be doing. We just didn't know *how*. You have actually *done* it, and you are showing us how." With that declaration, we had our first government-level commitment to take the

People's Planning Process and the inclusive governance process forward, and with his presence—despite a busy official schedule, Minister Kai-Kai stayed with us in Taiama for the full three days—we trusted the depth of that commitment even more.

John and I celebrated this moment of acknowledgment and commitment to the PPP from the government. We knew it heralded a new phase of opportunity, and we also knew that it represented the *beginning of* this next level of growth, much more than it delivered a conclusion about it. We knew that the process of securing full government buy-in and national implementation would be long and arduous, and that we would encounter risks and unknowns at every turn. And we also knew that even with Minister Kai-Kai's full and immediate support, the successful implementation of people- and community-led peace and development had to grow *from the inside out*—even when rolled out nationally. Without strong local leaders holding the center of the process, we knew we risked losing it to the centripetal force of a fragmented, outside-in system. That would mean business as usual. We knew district leaders yearned for stronger national support of this kind of inclusive local leadership in peace and development, and we wanted them to lead and drive the process so that they could counter the pressure of the status quo.

That meant our next commitment in living into this inside-out system was the strengthening of the district-level bowl. The Inter-District Learning Conference had been conceived as a space for the district committees, the IDCs, to learn and share with each other, to strengthen their organism, and to plan the next phases of their work in their districts. This work was, in fact, the heartbeat of our time together, at least for the first two days of the conference.

The first day included jam-packed presentations by each IDC about their first year of work, which seeded later reflection, integration, and planning within and across districts. Their stories and ideas offered direct learning to each other, and even more so, the spirit and the process they expressed and saw reinforced each IDC's self-confidence and commitment. All of this, in turn, became a subtext of the learning for the global audience.

The Koinadugu IDC described coming together to address youth violence by mediating a latent conflict between youth and the national government that had erupted into violence in their district. In Nieni Chiefdom, the people had raised enough money from the community to begin building three critically needed bridges, without waiting for their local government. Almost shamed into action, the district council had then offered the engineers and final supplies. In Kailahun District, traditional and elected leaders had committed to forging an agreement to forestall future conflict between them. Women, meanwhile, had assumed new leadership roles. Though everyone had warned the district leadership that men simply wouldn't follow a woman's leadership, the female vice-chair of the district led successful meetings when the (male) chair was absent. In Moyamba, the IDC committed to raising its own funds so that its work would not be dependent on outsiders, and it forged a new revenue-sharing agreement, addressing one of the toughest obstacles to effective local governance in Sierra Leone. The IDC process and the structure it was part of enabled district leaders to deal directly with even the thorniest issues. With the trustworthy container of an inclusive, self-determining process, they were able to solve these challenges *themselves*.

In my conversations with John, I'd heard about many of these accomplishments already. But witnessing the IDC representatives talk about the issues and how they addressed them, owning their significance and value, brought it home in a different way. I felt like I wasn't hearing *about* something, or merely watching or supporting it from the outside. In that room, all of us, including me, were *experiencing* it directly. It felt like a precious immersion, once again, into a healthy, vibrant, growing organism. And I was acutely aware of the lived creativity this organism was expressing—the "moral imagination" embodied, with powerfully creative ideas and action emerging from and speaking to the hard realities of people's day-to-day lives.

The spirit of ownership embodied in these conversations was evident and inspiring. "We are not expecting outside funds to come into our districts until we take responsibility for ourselves," said Alex Bonapha, then the district council chair in Kailahun and later the head of the Decentralization Secretariat in the Ministry of Local Government and Rural Development, the initial command center for implementing the national framework that grew out of this event.

Sheku Kamara, then the district council chairman and chair of the IDC in Koinadugu, crystalized a sentiment expressed by everyone there: "Fambul Tok has shown us we are able to take development into our own hands." And it was more than a sentiment; he reframed it as a guiding question for the IDC's learning and action. During the intradistrict reflection time, Chairman Kamara asked the Koinadugu group to reflect in personal, immediate terms: "What can my council and this IDC do *now*?" In answering, the group identified immediate priority needs and took responsibility for moving things forward in a grounded way that connected to the larger national vision.

Dr. Bob Kandeh, the district council chair and IDC chair in Moyamba, committed his district to taking responsibility for spreading the PPP to other chiefdoms "without needing other outside resources." Though Fambul Tok itself was technically an outside resource and would play a role in helping spread the PPP, the chairman's words expressed the depth of ownership the IDCs felt and the level of commitment that flowed from that ownership. They were committing to doing *their part* of the process fully without waiting for someone to do it for them or to give them permission to do it.

Hearing these stories, and witnessing the spirit of their sharing, in turn strengthened the resolve of everyone present. It was directly feeding and nourishing us.

That nourishment would bear fruit beyond our wildest imaginings. Mere months after our meeting in Taiama, the commitment that grounded and connected everyone there would formalize as the Wan Fambul National Framework for Inclusive Governance and Local Development (WFNF). Officially adopted as policy by the government of Sierra Leone in 2018, the Framework survived an election, a change in national government, and multiple leadership changes in all the relevant ministries. Since then, national legislation has been revised to reflect the PPP and IDC infrastructure, to make sure it is ensconced in law. The Framework has been integrated into the country's key development plans and its national budget. With all the necessary plans and agreements in place, the focus now is on funding to roll the work out nationally. Fambul Tok hosts the Secretariat that supports the Framework, tending both the work and the spirit of the new system being built, a system dedicated to recognizing and building on the very real resources already present in the culture, the people, the commitment, and the capacities across Sierra Leone.

The work, the vision, the faith, and the commitment it took to get there are nothing short of extraordinary. But the idea, and the possibility itself, had always existed. It was simply waiting to be claimed and forged into expression.

Perhaps no one saw this more clearly that day in Taiama than Chief Foday Alimamy Jalloh, the paramount chief from Nieni Chiefdom, whose people began building three bridges with nothing more than their own desire. As he said, powerfully and simply, "When the people are resolved, nobody stops them."

Chapter 17

GROUNDING IN SPIRIT

An important part of the national conference was the groundwork we did in the lead-up to it, led in important ways by and for women.

For years, Lilian Morsay, the national director of Fambul Tok's Peace Mothers program, had voiced a strong yearning to create a space where Peace Mothers from different districts could teach and learn from each other, consistent with the approach embodied throughout Fambul Tok's programming. She had cultivated a systematic approach to identifying and mentoring individual women leaders, but she had a vision for a more collective, programmatic cultivation as well. Though embedding the Peace Mothers program within Fambul Tok was a core part of its strength, success, and community impact, this very embeddedness also meant that the Peace Mothers program didn't have a singular focus on strengthening its programming. We knew from experience that bringing people from different locations together in person strengthened the work on the ground exponentially. These gatherings activated and made visible the larger whole that connected otherwise isolated communities, and magnified the learning and leadership of those communities. An invitation to share your wisdom and skills with others was a source of immense pride, which then reflected and spread out over the whole community. We wanted to activate this for the Peace Mothers program as a whole.

We also recognized that getting women's equal representation on IDCs had been difficult, despite Fambul Tok's commitment to valuing their voices. Most of the committees' membership was allocated for key elected and appointed local government offices, which were still heavily male. So the majority of IDC executives attending the IDL Conference were going to be male, and the presence of national government officials and international leaders would add to the likelihood that men would be the dominant voices in the room.

We decided to host a national Peace Mothers conference, and we scheduled it the day before the IDL in order to prepare women leaders at the community and district levels to participate more fully in the IDL event. We also loved the idea of having the Peace Mothers' energy sanctify the space with a spirit we envisioned carrying into the IDL event.

Amy and Lilian worked together closely to prepare the gathering. Lilian had in turn tapped three other Fambul Tok staff members to help. She knew Zainab, Lucia, and Fatim (yes, *that* Fatim) would excel in identifying, coordinating, and preparing the participants from across Fambul Tok's areas of operation. She also wanted to train and mentor them into new levels of national leadership—yet another expression of Fambul Tok's nested circles of invitational leadership development at work.

Although having a planning committee scattered across the country made the preparation even more difficult than it otherwise would have been, that commitment to growing new leadership was worth the extra time, energy, and expense. On the morning of the conference, as they stood in the courtyard across from our meeting room, Lilian, Zainab, Lucia, and Fatim positively glowed with pride, excitement, and strength. And after the months of planning and the days of travel, seeing their radiant presence that first morning was a gift and a balm, a reminder of the substance and power of what had *already* been accomplished simply through preparations for the event.

The feminine at the center

There were Peace Mothers in attendance from all six districts that Fambul Tok had worked in, including districts where it was no longer active but where the Peace Mothers still continued their work—an illustration of the power of the idea, the women, and Fambul Tok's way of working. As was often the case in Fambul Tok's convenings, many of the women who came to Taiama had never been outside their section or their chiefdom, much less their district. To the twin conferences (Peace Mothers and Inter-District Learning), we had also invited international women, including Dr. Tecla Namachanja Wanjala, who had chaired Kenya's Truth, Justice, and Reconciliation Commission; Angi Yoder-Maina, founder and executive director of the Green String Network, which pioneered a locally led trauma healing process in

East Africa; and Nyambura Mundia, a gifted young Kenyan leader and organizer. We had leading peace and human rights practitioners and scholars from Guatemala, the Democratic Republic of Congo, Germany, and the Netherlands, who represented governments, NGOs, UN agencies, and universities. They had come as listeners and learners and were immediately swept up as sisters by the Sierra Leoneans, who were both touched and inspired that women were coming from other countries to learn from them.

We also appreciated the presence of two compassionate male leaders and listeners, Charles and John. Charles has dedicated his life to supporting the leadership of women, and he had been an important partner and supporter to Amy in the planning and preparation for the conference. But sharing his belief that what was most needed now was a truly women-led and female-normed space, Charles told Lilian he would be happy to support the event from outside the space. She replied, "Of course you will be in the conference with us! We will christen you Charlestina. And John will be Johnette. You will be honorary women!" And so, Charlestina and Johnette lived the reality of the inclusivity of women's leadership, joining as men in support roles. This presence added even more depth and power to the day.

After double-checking the room setup, Amy, Charles, and I were ready to begin and starting to wonder where all the Sierra Leonean women were. Just then, Lilian appeared and invited us into the courtyard outside. As we walked out into the morning sun, women in gloriously colorful dresses and headwraps began singing and dancing their way over to us from across the courtyard, many holding signs of welcome and messages of gratitude for Fambul Tok and Catalyst for Peace, or carefully printed messages of the power of women and the people of Sierra Leone. The Peace Mothers wanted to begin the conference *their* way, and even though we had technically invited them to the conference, they wanted to welcome *us* to their land and their home. They were claiming their space and their leadership from the beginning. The group eventually circled and encompassed us all, and we became one big singing, dancing, joyful organism.

Being surrounded by these women—by their songs and their energy and their messages of power and of gratitude—felt like an injection of sanity and hope, of joy and freedom. It was impossible not to be lifted up by them. Eventually the singing subsided, as one of the women initiated a call-and-response of what had emerged as the anthem of the Peace Mothers.

"WOMEN!!!" she yelled loudly to the group, who then responded in unison, "**POWER!!!**"

Then again: "WOMEN . . . *POWER*!!"

And finally: "MEN . . . *SUPPORT*!!"

It felt as if their cheer both conjured and reinforced that power. And we sure needed it at that moment. The national Peace Mothers conference was held on November 9, 2016, the day after Election Day in the US. Charles, Amy, and I had gone to sleep the night before confident that our country was electing its first female president. In the lead-up to the Peace Mothers conference, I had imagined we would bring some special kind of legitimation to the day, representing a country that just elected its first woman president. In my imagination, that felt like a neat bookend to the lived example of grassroots, collective power the Peace Mothers represent.

Instead, we stumbled out of our rooms in shock and disbelief, falling into each other's arms and choking back tears, not always successfully. I don't think it's an overstatement to say that the women of Sierra Leone saved us that day. With their celebratory welcoming, the Peace Mothers were expressing their thanks to us for this chance to be together, to learn from each other, to encourage each other, to celebrate with each other, and to feel part of a national and international community of women change leaders. But I think we needed *them* much more than they needed us at that moment.

With something as seemingly simple as opening the day together and with song, these women were inviting us all into our best selves, and they were showing us what's possible when we come together in that desire. Listening to their cheer, receiving their joyful, anticipatory welcome, I had a flash that maybe the rural women of Sierra Leone stepping into their full power was actually an example of the kind of embodied feminine power the world *most* needed.

In many ways, I felt a parallel between this gathering and the Fambul Tok bonfire ceremony in Bomaru, where the women of Bomaru had inaugurated their cleansing ceremony with dance, circling their sacred rock and establishing their presence at the heart of their community's healing process. These women had broken with tradition, staking claim on a *new* tradition that honored both their wartime loss and their postwar leadership potential. The conference center at Taiama wasn't a sacred rock, and the upcoming Inter-District Learning Conference wasn't a community cleansing ceremony. But seeing the women sing and dance the space to life with messages of power and gratitude felt like a parallel reclaiming of the collective sacred, broadly defined, and of women's place at the heart of it. By sanctifying the space this way, the Peace Mothers were not only reclaiming and rearranging some of

Sierra Leone's public space for and by women, but also living into a sacred heart-center of peace and development for them and, really, for the world.

Once again, the feminine was at the center, and she was singing and dancing.

Preparing the ground

The Peace Mothers event opened and held space that helped ensure our deeper values grounded the full conference. And it was only part of how Amy, Charles, and I had brought intentionality to creating the container for the gatherings of that week.

We had been preparing for the twin conferences for several months, including with weekly calls with John and his team. The spirit of genuine partnership and mutuality of those calls, even more than their agenda, held power. They exemplified the fertile soil and robust root network we were creating and enriching, as part of our work together more generally but for these conferences in particular.

Both CFP and Fambul Tok have always practiced planning as more than a linear list of to-dos and mechanistic box-ticking toward an objective. We've used checklists and ticked boxes, to be sure. But we have—deliberately—created and inhabited a way of moving into and through activities that isn't merely about *accomplishing* things; it's about *listening* for what needs to and what wants to happen next, with a sensibility of organic emergence, which requires listening for and tuning to a larger wisdom. We do this because we situate ourselves as *already within* a whole and healthy, regenerative system, individually and collectively, and we are listening to and for how to move forward from that place and with that alignment.

As part of our ongoing Wisdom Circle work, we have each felt and held responsibility for doing this individually, and we have practiced it collectively. As a regular Catalyst practice, when we are heading into a significant event or activity, we take time to reflect on what success in that activity would look like to us, personally and more generally. Charles, Amy, and I first do that individually, and then we share our ideas with each other. Inevitably there are many commonalities, which is powerfully reinforcing. The distinct contributions of each person also expand and enrich the visioning for us all, enabling us to see the larger whole in new ways. We use this practice as part of our spiritual support and as part of how we hold the space for the event.

Even with such a disciplined practice of listening for and trusting Spirit, the first morning of the IDL Conference was not without discomfort about the uncertainty of the event ahead of us. We knew we needed the government on board in order to scale nationally, and we also knew how easily government engagement might co-opt the work for partisan and political purposes, or might otherwise divert, dilute, or corrupt what we had built. We had also taken new risks by inviting outside leaders. These included delegates from UN agencies and USAID, and from civil society in Liberia, Guinea, Kenya, and Congo. We invited them not as "experts" to offer insight from on high but as *listeners and learners*. At one level, that felt brazen, bordering on impertinent. At another, it felt like the most natural and true and right thing to do. CFP and Fambul Tok together had long been embodying and calling for equal, mutually healthy relationships between insiders and outsiders and for two-way flow of ideas and resources between them. We were committed to bringing that same dynamic to the broader national/international relationship dyad. But doing so in practice, even in this small way, actually felt big and brave.

And we didn't really know how any of it would go. Would IDC executives from different districts feel open and curious with each other, or competitive and defensive? Would they be able to imagine and give shape to the national framework that would support the growth of their work across other districts? Would the minister of local government feel threatened by the power of what he saw, or would he recognize and embrace its purpose and potential? Would he even listen to it, or would he just give his speech and then leave without even engaging with the substance of what was actually present?

The Bigger Hand

It is customary in Sierra Leone for every meeting or event to begin with prayer, which John describes as reminding us all "who's really running the meeting." John and I have also found it helpful to start the day of an event with time for private prayer and reflection together, and Amy, Charles, and I always started our gatherings in the US with a sacred opening. Given the intensity of the preparations, it felt especially important for us to begin that first day of the IDL Conference with spiritual grounding. I knew John would welcome the time for prayer, for connecting to a deeper Source, and for reminding ourselves we were held by "the Bigger Hand."

The opening morning of the Inter-District Learning Conference, I invited him, Amy, and Charles to share prayer in my room, before breakfast and the rush of the day's events. I was so grateful for the depth of spiritual maturity and practical wisdom in our little group, as well as for the relationships of trust we had cultivated that opened us to being spiritual resources for each other and for the work at hand.

We arranged ourselves in an almost-circle in my sparse, cramped room. I could still feel the gratitude and inspiration from the Peace Mothers conference the prior day, alongside an expectancy about the next days and an awareness of their significance, which brought the sharp edge of uncertainty. I also sensed a heaviness in John, which I attributed to a combination of exhaustion from the preparations and a deep, well-earned wariness of working with the national government in a highly politicized country.

Not having a clear sense of how to start our time, I simply expressed my deep appreciation for all that had brought us to this point, and I noted the power and potential of the moment, along with its accompanying risk and uncertainty. With the weight John was carrying so clearly visible, I asked him if there was anything specific he wanted our support for.

John hesitated a moment, not sure if he could or should share. He shifted in his chair a bit, took a deep breath, and began to tell us that he had had a vivid dream—what felt like a nightmare, actually—and that it had left him disturbed and distressed. He grew quiet again, his shoulders slumped and his head bowed toward the floor. Charles invited him to share about the dream, if he wanted to and felt comfortable, and told him that if it was weighing so heavy in his thought, we were there to help him hold it.

In all our time working together, I'd never heard John mention a dream before. And given the ominous feeling it left him with,

I can only imagine how difficult it was to share. But he did. His mother had appeared to him in the dream, in a way that he worried was a warning about the dangers of the work he was about to embark on, specifically the potential work with the national government. After he described the vivid images of his dream, he again fell silent, head tenderly bowed, his face a measure lighter from simply sharing.

Expressing deep gratitude for the courage it took for John to share his dream with us, Charles invited us into a time of silent listening and prayer for John and for how to go forward. Charles has a beautiful way of creating a space that honors the deep difficulty of something while also supporting trust and receptivity to Spirit. Charles brought us out of our silence with an invocation that opened up a larger space of grace and Love to hold each of us, the work ahead of us, and everyone who was gathered for it.

Without missing a beat, Amy shared an interpretation of the dream that had come to her, one that illuminated a positive message of encouragement. It struck us all, and John specifically, as exactly right. We talked through how that message might speak to the concerns we, and especially John, had about the day.

In the quiet time, a song I had been listening to that morning came singing back to me, so I played it for the group, and it became the perfect closing to our time together. Bobby McFerrin's "The 23rd Psalm" is distinctively beautiful. He also uses the feminine throughout, singing about God as Mother and using feminine pronouns.

All together, the whole was perfect. And not just for John—for all of us.

We didn't need to have that kind of thoughtful, prayerful time with everybody gathered for the event. But for the core leadership team, for our little group—his "tree," as John refers to us—it was important, powerful, and necessary. To have a safe space to share our deepest fears or our darkest visions, to have those held with patience and faith and trust and love, and to open to the invisible resources that are there to support us in moving through them was a gift. And it opened a space for a deeper, confident, trusting, receptive leadership.

No one could have created this experience alone. Each of us brought something different into the circle. It required trust and vulnerability for each of us to offer what we had, without knowing how the rest would unfold. I affirmed the value of starting our day with sacred time together and inviting everyone into it, without having any idea how it would go or what we would do. John brought his fear and his dream, and the courage to share them both. Charles invited and offered a way into prayer together that opened us to Spirit, right there. Amy received an interpretation of the dream that rang true and felt transformative and healing. The song I shared helped tie everything with grace and beauty. And we all helped hold the space and purpose with deep faith and trust, in each other and in the Bigger Hand, holding and guiding us.

Our shared spiritual grounding that first morning modeled a dynamic that was actually built into and throughout the whole Inter-District Learning event, not just our personal prayer time, and a dynamic across our work and approach more generally: no one—no one person, group, sector, or level of the system—could create the experience on their own. Everybody brought something, and what each person brought was different. Every piece comes together to form a larger whole; each piece is needed yet insufficient on its own. The shared purpose we hold together pulls us all forward, enabling the individual and communal transformation we need in this work—and in our lives—to unfold.

All together, the whole is perfect.

Chapter 18

INVITING WHOLENESS

T he third and final day of the IDL Conference was dedicated to imagining the way forward, building on the learning from the first two days of the conference. With a smaller group of core leaders from across the districts and the national and international landscapes, we began to imagine what a national platform that could support the growth of this work across the country might look like and how we might bring it into being. John and I wanted the IDC executives to lead that conversation so that their grounded, embodied wisdom would be the foundation for that national growth.

Everyone shared the desire to expand the PPP and inclusive governance process across the nation. "The IDC makes my job at least 60 percent easier," said Koinadugu District Council Chair Sheku Kamara, who was also chair of the IDC there. My eyes grew wide hearing him describe such a significant impact, given how often I hear that collaboration adds *extra* work. His words were incredibly gratifying, especially because I recalled his initial resistance and rather sour demeanor at the exploratory district stakeholder meeting. Since then, he had become one of the most active and personally involved IDC chairs. In fact, in the early months of the IDC pilot, he had been the first district council chair to call for a national infrastructure to support this work and roll it out nationwide. And now, he noted the dilemma that also accompanied that potential growth. "If we move too fast," he said to the group, "we risk losing the core values. How do we grow this in a way that we don't lose the core values, the spirit?"

I practically burst into tears at that comment. I actually had to cover my gaping mouth with both hands to prevent a spontaneous outburst. It wasn't his comment in and of itself, or even him saying it that moved me. His question, and the understanding and commitment behind it, confirmed how fully the leaders gathered had internalized the process and values we had been working for, and from, for years—values that John and I yearned so deeply to see grow as the norm for peace and development in Sierra Leone.

We knew from our experience that the *how* of the work was its real magic, even more than the *what* of it. It was the *how* that was creating the space for Musu Mohammed to own a room full of national and international dignitaries, for a government minister to say that this was the way he knew they were *supposed* to work, for a district council chair to feel his work was 60 percent easier. Growing the work was needed and important. But *how* that growth happened was most important. And we knew that only if leaders at every level internalized the *how* could a national platform that truly supported people and communities grow in the way it was most needed. In this moment, I saw that beginning, and it knocked my socks off.

I remembered the night of the second Fambul Tok bonfire, where I witnessed stunning examples of truth-telling, apology, and forgiveness in the village of Gbangbakordu. That night, I lay on the mat in the room I was sharing with Sara, but I just couldn't sleep. Replaying the evening left me tingling, my heart spilled over from all that was pouring into it. "I'm not sure I can hold so much good," I told Sara, my hands pressed up against my heart. I knew the Gbangbakordu ceremony was just the beginning of a much longer process, that there would be more of that goodness unfolding across the country. Aware of the incredible privilege of supporting something like that into being, I felt waves of gratitude overwhelm me.

I felt a parallel moment of watching something powerful, good, and true come into expression before me in the tiled-floor conference room in Taiama, and it filled me with gratitude. This, too, was just a beginning. I could glimpse what would and could be unleashed as it went forward, and I was again filled with a sense of awe at witnessing and supporting that as it happened.

An outside-in system would have been happy to build on a promising pilot, looking for the most rapid way to scale and assuming that it would guarantee results (or, conversely, that good results retroactively indicated good process). But an inside-out system honored the *how* and put it at the center of the system—a process that created space for people and communities, at every level, to listen for and lean into what *they* most wanted so that they could mobilize and bring it into being. We had succeeded together, starting from the most remote village and working outward, in redefining healthy growth—established in, and by, practice.

In that moment, I realized we had also managed together to redefine success. We weren't looking for scale or predetermined outcomes. Our indicators were less tangible and more important. We *were* looking for (and forward to) people and communities and their leaders stepping more fully into their potential—becoming, in essence, *more fully themselves*. That was true success in this system, and it was what we were seeing unfold in front of us, through people, process, and programming.

In *Mothering & Daughtering*, the book she wrote with her daughter Eliza, family therapist Sil Reynolds defines mothering as "raising your daughter to become herself."[8] It is perhaps not too much of a stretch to think that insights from nurturing individual development (aka parenting) apply to fostering *social* development as well, especially within an inside-out framework, grounded as it is in a desire to be and bring our whole selves, as people, and to be in healthy and mutual relationship with each other. As a parent, I have no greater joy than seeing my children being and becoming fully themselves in the world. I feel similarly as a supporter of international peace and development; I really cannot imagine a greater joy and professional (or personal) privilege than getting to watch people step into their capacity and leadership.

Redefining success as people and communities and their leaders becoming more fully themselves is important for international policymakers, funders, and other outsiders committed to supporting peace and development, and it requires us to change so much about how we work. From the first bonfire ceremony in Sierra Leone

---

8   Eliza Reynolds and Sil Reynolds, *Mothering & Daughtering: Keeping Your Bond Strong through the Teen Years* (Louisville, CO: Sounds True, 2013), 35.

to this global conference, we had structured a process around the goal of fulfilling people and communities' potential. That framing required different ways of working at every level.

But in the communities we support, this redefinition is more fundamental, more viscerally transformational. As one of the IDC chairmen explained, talking about the PPP, "The people feel they are no longer beggars, because this comes from the people."

When you lead peace and development from the inside out, the transformation you're working for begins as soon as you begin the work, and that transformation happens in every direction, including inwardly, in the self. I had learned that I could only be comfortable with and within a system that—on some level, at least—wanted the same for me, as a funder in that system, that it wanted for a Peace Mother from Peje Bongre Chiefdom. "Fulfilling potential" is invitational for villagers facing Ebola *and* for global donors wanting to help build peace. And I was finding and inhabiting that system of mutuality—or perhaps building it *by* inhabiting it—from the inside out.

A living learning space

Amy, who was once my student, said later that our four days in Taiama had been like "seeing Libby in her classroom." It wasn't only that conference room, during that week, that was my classroom. It really had been the whole work and program over the years; the Inter-District Learning event was just a culminating moment, a moment of reveal.

The classroom is actually a resonant metaphor for the substance and power of our whole way of working. We had created a living learning space where we could live into a new way of being together in this work, learning along the way how to do it. The frame of "fulfilling potential" had invited us into this living learning space. Even as we all came from different places and held different roles, we were side by side, looking ahead together, asking how we could grow, and grow into, an inside-out system of peace and development in Sierra Leone. This can't be done in the abstract; it has to be done through action. And it isn't a one-time event but an ongoing, iterative process of living and learning the way forward.

That, in turn, means we need places and processes to support our living and learning. Everything we had done, from the beginning of my work with John to this very moment, had ultimately been about bringing that into fulfillment.

Committing to fulfilling potential, rather than focusing primarily on solving problems, reoriented not just the work in the districts but the conference room itself. It wasn't just community members or local leaders who came there to learn. We *all* were there as learners—including, especially, those of us representing the international policy and funding community. With the frame of fulfilling potential, and the invitation to be present as learners, not lecturers, we could be and bring more than just our analytical minds, our connections, our clout, our money—more than the tools normally used in the transactional dimensions of international work. We could—we had to—also bring our hearts and our souls. And that meant those parts of us could also be reached and transformed.

This reorientation catalyzed new vision, new connections, and new communities of learning and co-creation that would grow in the years ahead. Claudia Agreda, a human rights leader and scholar from Guatemala, said, "I don't know how I can give back what I am taking from you. I owe you. I am taking a new vision. I am taking all the wisdom of the women in my heart. I am taking all the knowledge, new tools." Angi Yoder-Maina, who was advising the Somali government on a national policy framework for supporting strong local governance, wrote, "You are making the intractable possible. Each of you, by taking ownership and by coming together. I want to bring the Somalis here to learn." Two and a half years later, she did just that, along with a team from Kenya, sponsored by the Mombasa County governor's office. Peter van Sluijs, coordinator for the UN-initiated Civil Society Platform for Peacebuilding and Statebuilding, said, "The energy in the room has caught my heart. When people don't feel connected, they get disheartened. Here, there is a connection made. People *feel* they can say what they think, what they want."

Taiama was a moment when the whole process—the wholeness of the process and the power that it unleashes—became visible.

That wholeness would come to hold so much more than we imagined that day. And once again, women led the way. The national Peace Mothers conference catalyzed a broader interest in gathering women peacebuilding leaders together globally, and we did just that in Kenya in early 2018. Lilian and her team brought a Peace Mothers delegation to the beautiful Kenyan coastal town of Malindi to share their stories and approach and to help support, celebrate, teach, and learn from women peacebuilding leaders from across the continent. Everyone was invited as both an expert and a student, from whatever level of the system—local leaders, national policymakers, funders, practitioners—and all were equally valued. We centered women's ways of knowing and relating, celebrated the gifts of local networks of care, and honored the hard-won wisdom of laboring from deep inner knowing even when the status quo feels like an immovable obstacle to success. The gathering affirmed the sensibilities we all brought to our work across diverse settings, and we all went home strengthened and supported in decision-making, organizing, and governance.

The learning-in-practice space expanded from there. In 2019, we hosted more than 125 peace and development practitioners from around the world for a weeklong immersive learning event in Sierra Leone that we called Constellating Peace from the Inside Out. Vertically integrated teams, from local community to national civil society to national government to funder, came to Sierra Leone from Afghanistan, Somalia, Kenya, and Zimbabwe, alongside leaders from Northern Ireland, the United States, the Netherlands, and across Sierra Leone. As in Taiama, the *whole system* was represented, and the system itself was an explicit focus of discussion. Learning-in-practice, across sectors and across countries, inspired everyone, all the more so because such an opportunity is rare. Once again, people felt their whole selves invited and the best of themselves called forward. The global "bowl" became more visible, as the event fulfilled its name, constellating a global community of practice from the inside out. That community continues to grow and strengthen.

Although whole-body, whole-person, whole-system learning experiences are too rare in international peacebuilding and development, leaders crave that kind of experience. I have seen these events and the person-centered approaches they embody slake a deep thirst for working differently—working without feeling impelled by externally defined systems and structures and instead being motivated by the highest and best wisdom from within the self and within the local context. People are yearning to trust, to lean into, and to learn from their own embodied knowledge and experience, their own wisdom. And when we create spaces that invite and support that, and when we include people from diverse settings, we create opportunities for new kinds of learning and growth. These are the experiences that can truly transform—people, communities, and countries.

AND NOW

Head to heart

They say that the longest distance in the world is the distance from the head to the heart. I think that's true both individually and systemically. For Fambul Tok and Catalyst for Peace, Taiama was a moment where that distance was bridged. When I heard Peter van Sluijs's comment, it drove that reality home for me.

"The energy in the room has caught my heart. When people don't feel connected, they get disheartened. Here, there is a connection made. People *feel* they can say what they think, what they want."

Peter's comment completed a circuit for me. He wasn't only talking about rural Sierra Leoneans; he was also referring to himself and to other "internationals" present. And to everyone in the system, really. Peter saw and felt the connection we were making between sectors, and he identified the real root of that connection, of the desire and drive to connect: the human heart. The wholeness of the system isn't just about all sectors being present; it is about the wholeness of people being invited. Head, heart, hands, feet . . . People were invited, and were present, in their full humanity, not just in their role in the peace and development and governance system. At Taiama, we activated and made explicit the connection between our lived lives and the aid and development systems we use to support social progress. With our hearts invited and centered, we, too, could lead from the inside—*our* inside—out.

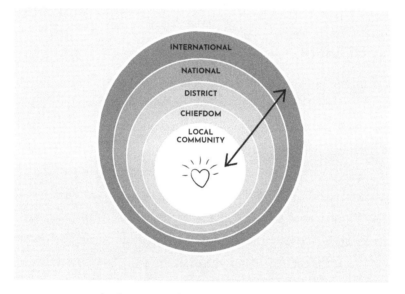

At the center of it all—the human heart.

We are—all of us, always—invited to be heart-whole, as well as system-whole. And when we are, it completes the circuit from the inside out, and back again.

If repairing the communal cup unleashes new energy and capacity for communal work, then what is possible when the *vertical* connections are repaired? When living bridges connect the levels and sectors of a system, and communal norms welcome, honor, and engage the heart?

When the heart is at the heart of it all, we find and feel new energy. We connect feeling to thinking to desire. That's the connection that "heartens," that shows us the heart is present and activated. Fambul Tok and Catalyst for Peace have lived and worked from that heart-center throughout, and Taiama made that visible in a new way.

Living justice

I've spoken about Fambul Tok in schools across the United States, and any time I've asked American students for images they associate with justice, or that represent their understanding of justice, they mention things like Lady Justice, the blindfolded woman holding scales who symbolizes the idea that justice is impartial and universal. Or they'll describe an imposing building with steep steps and tall pillars out front, the place where justice is dispensed, usually by an intimidating figure wearing a robe and sitting behind a high desk. Or the gavel that judges use to manage unruly crowds. And where do the principles of justice come from? Books, past precedents, the Constitution—formal doctrines and documents, many of them housed in those pillared buildings.

Sierra Leoneans' answers to the same questions could not be more different. When they describe justice, they often speak of people sitting together under a tree. *All* kinds of people—young and old, male and female, able-bodied and otherwise. From this perspective, justice is something that happens in informal spaces, spaces that are accessible to all. It happens in relationship and through conversation, together with your community. The authority undergirding this kind of justice comes from the community itself and from trust in a larger communal wisdom, rooted in lived experience, ancestral guidance, and common humanity.

That's why a tree is the central image in Fambul Tok's logo. The tree is a freely available gathering space. It is literally rooted in the earth and part of the natural world, and its presence has a community-establishing power. The tree is more than just the symbol of the place that holds communal justice. The deep roots, the sturdy trunk, the shade-providing branches, and the people gathered beneath them together make up the tree's presence and identity, its very life. People and tree together are living community.

John often refers to me, and our little inner circle of me and Amy and Charles, as his "tree." A place he can rest under and lean on, a place that helps him reconnect with his own deeper wisdom and the larger wisdom that holds him, and us. That offers a tangible, embodied reminder of the larger whole we are part of, together. And it hints at the nature of the larger whole we were building and inhabiting in our work—that, like a tree, it has and gives life. A living entity, made up of both the ideas we were working with and on, and ourselves, as people and leaders. And there is something of the miraculous in that. For me, a big part of the wonder of what we were creating and living into in Sierra Leone is quite simply its aliveness, as manifested in the space it offered for us to be and bring our whole selves and for the work and the structures that support it to grow and adapt with the people and their needs. Our work is an expression of a system as a *living organism*, as the metaphors of wombing and being wombed illuminated.

Living bridges

I recently learned about the strangler figs in northeast India. In the Meghalaya region of India, heavy annual rainfalls turn many streams and gorges into fast-flowing torrents of water and dangerous, impassable rivers. The prolific rubber fig tree has adapted a secondary root system that grows above ground, keeping the trees standing on top of the boulders or even in the middle of streams and rivers. Centuries ago, the Khasi and Jaintia peoples of the region discovered they could manipulate and direct these roots to create a bridge across the rivers and gorges, making them crossable even during the height of the summer rains. The process can take well over a decade of splicing and directing, binding and weaving, coaxing and strengthening, before a functional bridge grows into place. A finished bridge can be more than 150 feet long and easily bear the weight of 50 or more people. Some of these bridges are more than 500 years old.

The end result is truly a *living bridge*. And just like anything living, these bridges require strengthening and tending for generations to come. The trees themselves take care of the bulk of that regenerative process, as part of their natural cycles. In fact, as living bridges, they actually *strengthen* over time. But in Meghalaya, this natural process is accompanied and supported by the nurturing attention of the community.

Given how long the process takes, one generation may not ever see the fruits of its labors in a finished, usable bridge. The binding and weaving techniques are passed from generation to generation, and the longer-term vision and purpose is all they need to inspire them. The result is an astonishing network of bridges—and of the communities that made them. The knowledge of how to build them is held by so many people in the community that the practice and tradition seem as stable as the bridges themselves.

The work of growing Fambul Tok, from the most local level to the global one, has been a lot like weaving those living bridges. The patient coaxing and tending of roots across otherwise impassable distance resonates with the work we have done in building peace and development from the inside out. Individually, John and I are each rooted deeply in our own geographic and cultural contexts, on opposite sides of the Atlantic Ocean. The historic connections of those geographies have been so deeply destructive to human life and human dignity that the distances between us have been nigh on unforgeable. We have, however, unfurled and channeled, wound and woven, our own secondary root systems—the values and commitments we hold in common that transcend space, time, class, and culture. As we deepen and true to those individually, we have woven them into our leadership and into the work we have done together, the things that have formed the basis of our partnership over the last fifteen years. We have built a metaphoric root bridge across the Atlantic Ocean, a living bridge connecting an African civil society leader and an American funder, and the sectors we each in part represent, in mutually enriching and life-giving ways.

Now it's time to widen and expand that living bridge. I want others to use, to weave, and to strengthen the bridge of healthy, mutual teaching and learning; of an inside-out system of peace and development. At Catalyst for Peace, we want to see a network of living bridges.

As bridge-building goes, there's no halfway. A tightly woven, sturdy bridge requires the roots, and the weavers, to travel the full distance of the chasm. We all need to allow ourselves to be carried further than we've ever been. That is deeply relational work. And it is an ongoing conversation. The Latin root of conversation, *convers*, means "from the inside out," which seems especially fitting. "Like the living bridge between two riverbanks," author and educator Toko-pa Turner writes, "our conversation is the practice of belonging together."[9] Our fingers touch and our elbows bump as we weave our root cords—tendrils of vision, of affection and appreciation, of hard truths and courageous conversations, and ultimately of invitation and offering together.

Our conversation is the work of inhabiting the system of wholeness, the system where we each equally belong, and where our interactions are mutually nourishing and help us all step into our potential.

The invitation

Locating ourselves—centering and grounding ourselves—within an inside-out system asks something of us. It changes our fundamental orientation to our work. It requires us to put down any focus on "changing the system," as if the system were something separate from us, something "out there." It requires us to leave behind the idea that we are building and creating something new; we must, instead, *become* something new. This might still involve building and creating, of course. But in the work of becoming, we are full participants; we are *all in*, not somewhere outside of and separate from the work we are doing or the system we are building. And

---

9   Toko-pa Turner, *Belonging: Remembering Ourselves Home* (Salt Spring Island, BC: Her Own Room Press, 2017), 18.

there is no such thing as "finished," really. The work of becoming, like the tending of a living bridge, is always ongoing; it requires embracing ongoing process and not mere product. That, in turn, means constantly moving into the unknown. We need to be willing to be surprised, to not be in control, to be part of a larger whole, to watch, to offer, to trust, to change.

To facilitate our becoming, we must let go of ideas of strong leadership centered around knowing the most and having all the answers, presumably in order to give them to everyone else. When we invite our imagination instead of just our intellect, our faith and trust instead of just our grit and grind, our alongside-ness instead of our above-ness—when we welcome those things, we open channels for new creation to spring forth. Fambul Tok taught me the generative power of not knowing, especially when we trust the larger wisdom, the wisdom of the whole—when we trust that we can access it, and when we make space for it.

I want to invite you, and everyone interested in leading positive social change, to imagine what *you* want to make space for. To listen for your own markers of a whole and healthy system, and then choose to do everything you can to inhabit that system *now*. That's how to build peace from the inside out. To act *as if* the system were whole and healthy, and to work—to design programs, allocate budgets, hire and promote, partner and create—from there. How can you do your own work fully from within *that* system, the system you believe *should* be, right now, right where you are? How can you ask for, build, and inhabit circles of support for that system, beginning at the most local, immediate, personal level—right where you are?

What would it mean to live in a system of wholeness right now? What stirred in your soul as you read this book? Let that guide you toward your answer now. We need to listen to our soul-stirrings. To honor them. Our souls know how to do that. Our souls are whispering. Or yelling. To get us to listen and pay attention to our deepest desires. The world's soul is calling. The *anima mundi*. Let's listen. Let's help each other to listen. Let's follow, and let's help each other to follow.

As big an idea as that is—to live in a whole and healthy and life-giving, regenerative system *right now*—the way into it is actually small and intimate. We need to seek out the inner circles of wisdom in our own lived contexts and the people who can support us in connecting to that lived wisdom.

One of the most obvious lessons to me from my international peacebuilding journey is that small acts of care and nurturing, when supported and connected, can be centrifugal. Over and over again, in my personal life and in the work, I've seen that what we give, we make more of. Intimate, local networks of care are spaces of great power—places where we come together regularly to help others thrive and, in the process, create more good for ourselves. The *fambul*, not just in its biological but in its expansive communal meaning, is a powerful container. These close-in circles supporting us in being and becoming our highest and best selves are the circles (or trees) we each need in order to be and become our best selves.

Those of us with financial resources have an opportunity and a sacred responsibility to use them with that awareness—to open up, to activate and make visible, and to honor the other resources that exist, even (especially) in the places deemed most desolate. Let's invite and use financial resources to value the *real* resources for peace—healthy and whole communities, tapped into their creativity, collaboration, caring, and commitment. The spaces that invite and nurture our hearts and heart-wholeness. And the networks of connection and ways of working that honor, activate, and support the flow of that capacity.

As we do, together we will be rewriting our global communal narrative. We can live, and write, a different story. We can live, and resource, a different system. We need to think about resources more broadly, and we need to use one resource—money—to serve and support the activation, creation, and flow of *new* resources, or resources that were previously unseen. When we are as willing to receive as we are to give, to be transformed as we are to transform, we create the channel for the greater flow of good in the world, in our own communities, and in the communities we seek to serve.

I want to connect with others who are building living root bridges across other unforgeable divides, working from an already-not-yet healthy and whole ecosystem, even when that runs counter to everything that they have been taught, or that the culture around us serves, sanctions, and celebrates. Who are the wholeness visionaries and practitioners? Those working at the living, spiritual, pioneering edge of their visions, their highest and best values, their soul-whispers, out into the world, in community with others?

This book is one way I'm reaching out my own roots to connect with the ecosystem of wholeness, the roots of which are often unseen, beneath the ground. How do we connect at the level of our root systems to nourish and strengthen the emergence and expression of the new, healthy system ready to spring forth?

We can start by declaring that intention.

I have seen and experienced the ways in which the wholeness of community already, always exists as a resource. It is not a goal to attain; it is already here, available to draw from and use. I invite it forward. What could that mean for us to work more fully from this place?

Let's learn our way forward together. Our soul is calling us.

I don't know what it will look like. I don't know how it will happen. I'm not even sure what to do next.

But I do know the answers are there.

AFTERWORD

Fifteen years after Libby and I first met, I am still stunned by what our work and our shared vision have produced. I have always believed in the power of ordinary people to tackle their toughest challenges and to heal their deepest wounds, and even to this day, it remains difficult for me to express how challenged and wounded that terrible war left all of us in Sierra Leone. It is a blessing that Libby believed as much as I did in the power of these ordinary, unknown people—and believed in me, and in herself, enough to commit to helping them transform their communities.

These people also transformed this country. The journey Libby has recounted, from the earliest reconciliation bonfires to a nationally scaled program for inclusive governance and development, was possible because they stepped into the space we helped create, a space for ordinary people to take charge of their lives, their communities, their futures.

When they do, the question then becomes: What next? How can we transform the ways governance and development have always been done so that ordinary people can truly lead from the spaces created for them?

The "we" here means all of us. It means ordinary people, who must show up with the willingness to trust that this process can withstand difficult conversation. That takes courage, time, and accompaniment, as this book has shown.

The "we" means government leaders at every level in Sierra Leone. Their usual ways of working lock them up in a bureaucracy that blocks their access to the voices and needs of real people. When those ways of working are unlocked, and there are open channels for a two-way flow of communication between the leaders and the people, the government is empowered to act on its good intentions—not only to do things for the people but also to do things that the people want and need. They can go beyond the quick wins, which we all understand that politicians need, and answer the call they feel to be true servants of the people.

And the "we" means the international community. In my life's work, I've seen the ways the international community works transform through the partnership between Fambul Tok and Catalyst for Peace. We have demonstrated that there is a different way of working; we have shown what it can accomplish. Most importantly, because of that lived experience, we know what it takes for the usual ways of working to transform—and thus to make our collective efforts truly transformative in the places we all seek to be of service.

It has been a unique challenge to bring a locally driven, nonpartisan process into partnership with a government. Making sure the work is not politicized in the eyes of the people can be difficult: politicians need to claim credit, to press their projects into campaigns and election cycles. But communities trust the Fambul Tok model because it isn't politics.

In Sierra Leone, the Wan Fambul National Framework is succeeding by giving space to everyone's needs. There is a National Steering Committee, composed of government ministers, and just below it sits the National Technical Committee, which consists of directors and technicians who review and advise on proposals channeled up from the local to the national level. In this way, we have found a process for bringing an apolitical program to the highest political officials, who lead the changes needed at the national level. In this balance is our way forward.

Finding this way forward has required patience, learning, and careful tending. As the lead strategist for the Framework, I have helped accompany this process in much the same way that Libby accompanied Fambul Tok. But our goal is that the Framework, too, grows roots deep and strong enough not to need us. As the Framework reaches many more places than Fambul Tok could have dreamed, I want every community to embody its spirit—to begin, with its partners, by knowing that the answers are already within them, and to forge the path they need for the future they most want.

—John Caulker
Freetown, Sierra Leone

ACKNOWLEDGMENTS

Like every other dimension of this work, this book has been surrounded and supported by a strong community for quite a long time. As have I, as its author.

First and foremost, this book wouldn't exist without Jina Moore. She accompanied me in the writing of it for close to two years—encouraging, inviting, discerning, appreciating, redirecting, bolstering, occasionally cajoling, and, of course, masterfully editing. She midwifed the book that was in me, ready and needing to be born, while also giving me what felt like a graduate education in writing itself. Her deftness in helping me navigate the creative process offered a gentle, powerful, and generative container for my in-process-ness. It helped the writing process to be singularly integrative for my own learning and growth. I wish every writer could have a Jina.

This book also wouldn't exist without Charles Gibbs. While I had worked on a book sporadically over the years, it wasn't until Charles and I decided to write something together that I was actually able to begin writing in earnest. That work became the springboard for this book. Charles's companioning and our early cowriting helped me break through the major block I had to writing *my* story and centering *my* thoughts, and made writing not only possible in ways it hadn't been before but also fun. I imagine all writers face strong inner critics, but mine has been rather herculean, and I couldn't be more grateful to have had someone of Charles's generosity of spirit and skill to accompany me to the point where I not only *had to* write my own book but also, in fact, knew I *could*.

Amy Potter Czajkowski's conviction of the need for me to tell my story, and the constancy of her belief in my capacity to do it, offered the invitation I needed to move to and through my discomfort on many an occasion. In the early years of our work together, she devoted time to helping me imagine and outline, in ways that were foundational, what a book could and should be. Not to mention the ways her process genius grounded so many of the learning and planning spaces that yielded the stories I write about in the book.

Braden Buehler has been a communications teacher-fairy for me for years now. Whether it was writing prompts to jumpstart me into telling my story or editing my early writing in ways that always helped me get out of my head, she is a true writer whisperer. Her positive energy, and her ability to be inspired by the work and ideas while also helping their expression sound and read and look better, has been consistently soul-nourishing.

So many people read versions of the manuscript, and their feedback shaped the writing in important ways. Besides those already listed, they include Craig Fleck, Cynthia Sampson, Bryan Martin, Karen Grayson, Daly Ngarambe, Lari Snorek, Nelly Mecklenburg, Khyber Farahi, Rasoul Rasouli, Clare Lockhart, and the team at

Euphrates Institute. Kathryn Davis's spiritual support was foundational across the time I wrote the manuscript. Beth Tener has been an invaluable companion in imagining how this book might go out into the world and fulfill its potential.

My family has been my anchor (and my learning lab) for everything in this book. My husband, Seth, skillfully and lovingly held down the home front while I traveled the world, which made it all possible. (Although I suspect the Foreside Tavern actually *was* the family dinner table when I was away . . .) My children—Caleb, Gabe, and Anna—have expanded my heart more than I thought humanly possible. They have grounded me, stretched me, inspired me, and just plain made life more fun. They make my heart sing . . . every day.

And, of course, John Caulker. None of this would be possible without your vision, courage, capacity, and commitment—and your generous, skillful partnership. John, "thank you" hardly seems adequate. I bow in gratitude and appreciation.

INDEX

ABOUT THE AUTHOR

Photo by Danielle Cohen

As the founder and president of Catalyst for Peace, Libby Hoffman creates space for those most impacted by violence and war to lead in building the peace and restoring social wholeness. For 15 years, she has focused her work in Sierra Leone, as co-founder, funder, and ongoing program partner of Fambul Tok (family talk), a postwar reconciliation program rooted in local culture and tradition. After the 2014 Ebola epidemic, she helped adapt the Fambul Tok approach into a national policy framework for people- and community-led planning and development; the framework has become a model for transformative partnerships between international donors, national governments, and civil society.

Libby produced the award-winning documentary film *Fambul Tok* and coauthored a companion book of the same name. A former political science professor at Principia College, she has degrees from the Fletcher School of Law and Diplomacy and Williams College. The mother of three grown children, she divides her time between southern Maine and Washington, DC.

**For more about Libby and her work,
visit libbyhoffman.com and catalystforpeace.org.**